Hollywood Doesn't Live Here Anymore

Hollywood Doesn't Live Here Anymore

by

Robert Parrish

Little, Brown and Company
Boston   Toronto

COPYRIGHT © 1988 BY ROBERT PARRISH

ALL RIGHTS RESERVED. NO PART OF THIS BOOK MAY BE REPRODUCED
IN ANY FORM OR BY ANY ELECTRONIC OR MECHANICAL MEANS,
INCLUDING INFORMATION STORAGE AND RETRIEVAL SYSTEMS,
WITHOUT PERMISSION IN WRITING FROM THE PUBLISHER, EXCEPT
BY A REVIEWER WHO MAY QUOTE BRIEF PASSAGES IN A REVIEW.

FIRST PAPERBACK EDITION

Library of Congress Cataloging-in-Publication Data

Parrish, Robert.
    Hollywood doesn't live here anymore.

    Includes index.
    1. Parrish, Robert.   2. Moving-picture producers
and directors — United States — Biography.   I. Title.
PN1998.3.P36A3   1988   791.43′023′0924 [B]   87-29694

ISBN 0-316-69255-7 (hc)
      0-316-69258-1 (pb)

    Lines from "People Will Say We're in Love" from the musical
    Oklahoma! by Richard Rodgers and Oscar Hammerstein II.
    Copyright © 1943 by Oscar Hammerstein II and Richard Rodgers.
    Copyright renewed. All rights administered by Chappell & Co.,
    Inc. International Copyright Secured. All rights reserved. Used
    by permission.

10   9   8   7   6   5   4   3   2   1

Designed by Robert G. Lowe

MV

Published simultaneously in Canada
by Little, Brown & Company (Canada) Limited

PRINTED IN THE UNITED STATES OF AMERICA

To Kathie

Sometimes it's more fun making a movie than to have made it.

— Robert Parrish
January 1, 1988

Contents

List of Illustrations

Preface

Of all the books I have read about the movies, the best ones have not been about the movies themselves, but about the people who make them. You can learn most of what you want to know about *The Informer, The Long Voyage Home, The Grapes of Wrath, My Darling Clementine,* and *The Quiet Man* by buying ten or twenty tickets and seeing the movies ten or twenty times or watching them on videocassettes at home. But you wouldn't learn much about John Ford and his unique way of putting those movies on the screen unless you knew him personally or read a book about him. The same goes for D. W. Griffith, Charlie Chaplin, William Wyler, Alfred Hitchcock, Jean Renoir, Orson Welles, King Vidor, Ernst Lubitsch, and other important movie-makers.

That's why, when John Ford died on August 31, 1973, I decided to write something about him in my book *Growing Up in Hollywood.* The book was not supposed to be *about* John Ford, but, because he made some great movies and influenced my growing up, it seemed natural to include him. So I wrote about Ford and some others, and when I was nearly finished, I discovered I had written more about Ford than about any of the others. I decided that his death was a good place to end my book: the end of a talented Irish rogue with five Oscars rounding out the only book I planned to write about the movies.

Then Sam Spiegel died. How could anyone who knew Sam let his death pass unnoticed? He was larger than life, and I had always taken it for granted that he was also larger than death. I was wrong, alas, and so starts book number two. It's not only about Sam Spiegel; it's also and again about growing up, but not only in Hollywood.

NOW AND THEN

Sam Who?

From the *New York Times*, Wednesday, January 1, 1986:

> Sam Spiegel, the Academy Award–winning producer of
> such motion pictures as "The African Queen," "On the
> Waterfront," "Bridge on the River Kwai," and "Lawrence
> of Arabia," died yesterday while vacationing on the
> Caribbean island of St. Martin. He was 84 years old and
> had homes on Park Avenue, in London, and on the
> Riviera.

So far, so accurate — "All the News That's Fit to Print"–
wise. And, also, so sad. *The Times* obituary goes on:

> Mr. Spiegel, the prototype of the . . . cigar-chomping . . .
> wheeler-dealer on the international film scene . . .

That's when I stopped reading the obituary. I defy the
editor or the obituary writer of the *New York Times* to tell me
when either of them saw Sam "chomp" a cigar. It just wasn't
his style. First of all, he was too much of a gentleman to be
caught "chomping" on anything, except maybe a script, a film
director, an actor, a studio head, a critic, or a banker from time
to time. But I never heard of him doing this in the presence of
a newspaper editor or an obituary writer. So much for the
inaccurate, routine ("Get me the obit file on Sam Spiegel")
New York Times report on the death of this extraordinary man.

Sam's life was far from routine. No one I know can tell his
complete, true story because he kept the many chapters of his
life compartmentalized, separate, secret. His close friends

didn't necessarily know his other close friends, though his affection for each was never in doubt.

He was loyal to the men he admired, and when they died, he was gallant to their widows. Ask Mrs. William Wyler, Mrs. Arthur Hornblow, Mrs. Irwin Shaw, or Mrs. Humphrey Bogart, to name a few.

I'm not sure he ever introduced Elizabeth Taylor to King Hussein of Jordan or Charlie Chaplin to the queen of England, but he knew many famous people and sometimes arranged (or permitted) them to meet in his presence. For example:

An impeccable lunch was being served on the terrace at Sam's house, Mas de l'Horizon at Saint-Tropez. The guests were Bob and Kathie Parrish, Princess Aliata, Countess Belanga, Willi Rizzo (husband of Elsa Martinelli, but on this day escorting the twenty-three-year-old Countess de Rambeau and her seven-year-old son Philippe de Rambeau), and Adam Spiegel, also aged seven.

SAM: We sailed from Saint-Tropez to Majorca, and while we were there, I heard that he was in Palma so I invited him aboard. He stayed for lunch and brought the queen back for dinner the next evening.

PRINCESS ALIATA: I find him charming.

RIZZO: He has a difficult job.

ADAM: Who, Daddy?

SAM: A friend of mine, Adam. Don't interrupt.

COUNTESS DE RAMBEAU: He comes to shoot at my parents' place every year.

ADAM: Who does he shoot, Daddy?

SAM: I know his father, too. They're both good friends of mine.

ADAM: Who, Daddy?

SAM: Wait second. Wait second. (*He turns his good ear to Adam.*) What is it, Adam?

ADAM: Who are you talking about?

SAM: The king of Spain.

ADAM: Oh, him.

Whenever I was with Sam, I could count on him to exasperate me and enhance my life.

As my wife and I entered the funeral home on Madison

Avenue, I was greeted by Adam, Sam's now seventeen-year-old son. He asked me to say something that his father might have liked. Here's what I said:

> I don't remember where I met Sam Spiegel, or when. What I do remember is that he has been an important part of my life, and my affectionate memories of him will be with me as long as I live.

Shortly after the successful release of *The Bridge on the River Kwai* in New York, I met David Lean, the director, on Madison Avenue. He said he had just come from a final meeting with Sam and that they had decided to go their separate ways. "Sam's going to London tonight," he said.

"And where are you going?" I asked.

"Darjeeling," replied David.

"Why?"

David lit a cigarette in the peculiar way he lit cigarettes. (He held it between his thumb and little finger of his left hand.) He inhaled deeply and said, "I looked at the map and saw that Darjeeling is as far away from London as you can be without getting closer again."

Several years later, I was working for Sam in London. David had the office next to me on the third floor of Horizon Pictures on Dover Street. He was preparing *Lawrence of Arabia*. We shared coffee breaks, telephones, secretaries, and gossip.

"How did you get back together with Sam?" I said one day.

"After Darjeeling," said David, "I spent two years working on the life story of Mahatma Gandhi. I finally realized that it was too tough for me, and I sat in the lounge of the Taj Mahal Hotel in Bombay and stared ahead." He sucked on his cigarette and reflected. "After a while I looked down and was surprised to see a pen writing on hotel stationery. 'Dear Sam,' it wrote. 'I have been working on the Gandhi project for two years, and, while I know it will eventually make a great film, I also know that it will never amount to anything without a great

producer. Will you please come in on it with me?
Yours, David.'

"I recognized my own handwriting and signature
and mailed the letter quickly, before I came to my
senses." He paused.

"Two weeks later," David said, "Sam appeared in
Bombay, and a week after that he had convinced me
to make *Lawrence of Arabia* with him." He sipped
his coffee and then said, "He's very persuasive, you
know."

David's wife was in Bombay and my wife was in
Los Angeles. Quite often, David and I would have
dinner together or with Sam, who came into my
office one day and said, "Why don't you and David
have dinner with me at Claridge's tonight?"

At the hotel, Sam said, "Come with me. I have to
go up to Ben Goetz's apartment for a minute."
When we got to the apartment, Goetz, Willy Wyler,
John Huston, and Mike Frankovich were playing
gin rummy. Sam sat down and was dealt into the
next hand. And the next. And the next. David and I
stood around like stable boys. When we reminded
Sam of our dinner engagement, he would say, "Just
a second. Just a second," and play another hand.

Finally, David said to me, "Let's go." We
sneaked out and decided to have a quiet dinner at
the Terrace Room at the Dorchester Hotel, a few
blocks away. As we walked over, we both ful-
minated about Sam. "He's impossible," said David.
"You bet," I agreed. "He invites us to dinner, then
gets involved in a goddamn card game. It's crazy."
"And this is not the first time," said David. "He
does this kind of thing all the time. Nothing is ever
easy with him." "He's impossible," I said.

When we finally arrived at the Terrace Room, we
were both exhausted from denouncing Sam for his
real and imagined faults. As we sat down at our
table, David said, "This is ridiculous. We're wasting a beautiful evening. I propose no more talk
about Sam. We'll order and then the first one who so
much as mentions his name after that has to buy the
dinner."

I agreed. David ordered an oily-looking artichoke

and I ordered a shrimp cocktail. When we finished, David ordered another artichoke and I ordered a glass of white wine. Then we both sat in silence.

After a while, David lit a cigarette and offered me one. He knew I didn't smoke. I said, "No thanks," and sipped my wine. We were sitting near the window and I noticed a number 2A red bus passing near the window on Park Lane. Silent minutes, which seemed like hours, passed.

Finally, David said, "OK, Bob. This dinner is on me. Did I tell you what Sam tried to pull on me this morning?"

"Sam who?" I said.

2

It's Not Quite Right Yet

I am grateful to Sam Spiegel for many things, not the least of which is his reintroducing me to England, a country I had learned to love during the war. He also revived my interest in working outside of Hollywood. I had already made some movies "off the backlot," and the work had appealed to me. When Sam offered me a job directing *Dangerous Silence*, a movie to be shot in London with Jack Lemmon and Peter Sellers, I jumped at the chance. We never got the movie made, but it was Sam who was responsible for the Parrish family's moving, bag and baggage, with two children (Peter, eight, Kate, two) and a beagle hound named Timmy, to London and, using that as a base, living some of the best twenty years of our lives.

During those twenty years I directed and/or produced some films that I liked and, as one critic wrote, "some that are easily forgettable," but, with one exception, a film I thoroughly disliked, I enjoyed almost every minute of every film. I worked on scripts with Eric Ambler, Daniel Fuchs, T.E.B. Clarke, Bill Bowers, Billy Wilder, Robert Ardrey, Irwin Shaw, and Robert Shaw, among others. I directed many fine actors and actresses, including Michael Caine, Rita Hayworth, Jack Lemmon, James Mason, Robert Mitchum, Gregory Peck, Anthony Quinn, Jean Seberg, and Peter Sellers. I traveled to international locations: Ceylon, Tobago, London, Trinidad, Mexico, Paris, Normandy, Rome, Barcelona, Portugal, Marseilles, Kashmir.

I worked with a number of producers, but Sam Spiegel was the wiliest, most intriguing, and most skillful. With his continental accent, and its overtones of Park Lane and Park Avenue, he could at one moment exude persuasive charm and, at the next, dismiss an idea or a person with one sharp word or look. He had a way of concentratedly listening to what he wanted to hear and cutting you off if you were telling him something he already knew or didn't want to know. Above all, he knew how to get his own way.

Sam Spiegel, Willy Wyler, and Billy Wilder had known each other in Europe before the war and remained close friends after they all became successful in Hollywood, where it's hard to stay friends, whether you knew each other in Europe or not. When I told Willy I was going to direct *Dangerous Silence* for Sam, he said, "He's a very good producer, maybe the best."
"Why haven't you two ever worked together?" I asked.
"Working for Sam is for young people," said Willy, "people with time to spare. It takes me a year to make a movie. Sometimes it takes Sam two years or more *not* to make a movie. That's because he knows how to live well and make a picture, or not make a picture, at the same time. You'll have the time of your life, but maybe you won't have a movie."
"Is that the only reason you haven't worked with him, the time factor?"
"No. The real reason is more complicated. I just can't afford it."
I knew Willy was a wealthy man, and I knew Sam could pay him whatever he asked. I also knew that Sam had wanted Willy to direct several pictures that he had produced, and Willy had always shied away.
"Sam is one of my closest friends," Willy went on. "If we make a picture together we won't be friends anymore. I can't afford to lose him. He's too valuable."

Dangerous Silence should have been made into a successful movie. We had a good jewel-robbery thriller written by Donald McKenzie, a bona fide ex–jewel thief. We had Jack Lemmon and Peter Sellers, two top comedy actors. Four of the best screenwriters in the business had worked on the script.

And we had Sam Spiegel, a very good producer. I knew he was good because Willy had told me and also because every time Sam was shown a script, he said, "It's not quite right yet."

Sam submitted each of the first three scripts of *Dangerous Silence* to Lemmon and Sellers and they approved all of them. I approved them too, but Sam kept saying, "I want you to have the best possible script. It's not quite right yet."

As he was telling me this in his London office one day, his secretary interrupted on Sam's amplifier phone.

"It's Mr. Billy Wilder calling from Bad Gastein," she said. Billy had been taking the waters and playing gin rummy with Sam Goldwyn at the Austrian spa. Goldwyn had returned to Hollywood and Billy was lonely. He asked Sam to join him.

"How can I join you when I'm preparing two pictures?" said Sam.

"What are the pictures?" asked Billy.

"Bob Bolt and David Lean are working on the script of *Lawrence of Arabia,* and Bob Parrish and I are working on *Dangerous Silence.*"

"Is there anything I can do to help?"

"Yes, you can come to London and polish the script with us."

"I've got two free weeks," said Billy, "but I'm not going to spend them in London. If you can get me a suite on the top floor of the Hôtel de Paris in Monte Carlo, I'll meet you there." It was the height of the season and Billy knew he was asking the impossible, but he liked to put Sam on.

Sam said, "I'll call you back." He told his secretary to get two suites and a double room at the Hôtel de Paris. "If we can get Billy for two weeks, we'll have a great script," he said to me.

After a few minutes, Sam's secretary came in and said, "The hotel is booked solid. I talked to Monsieur Girard and he said he could promise nothing for ten days. He said he was very sorry."

"Get me Mr. Wilder in Bad Gastein," said Sam. When Billy came on the phone, Sam said, "It's all set. We'll meet you at the Hôtel de Paris on Monday." He paused for a moment and said, "Yes, the top floor. The royal suite." He hung up and said to his secretary, "Get me Prince Rainier on the phone."

*　　*　　*

The royal suite at the Hôtel de Paris is luxury all the way. Even a double room down the hall is not bad.

Billy set the ground rules the first night at dinner. "Here's the only way I know how to work," he said. "We start at eight in the morning, having had breakfast. We then work until six, with one hour out for lunch. That way we'll be too tired to go to the casino at night, and we'll all save money."

The next day Billy and I started at 8:00. At 10:30 Sam came in in his dressing gown. "How are you boys doing?" he said. We said we were doing fine. Billy asked Sam if he was going to work with us or just interrupt from time to time, and Sam said, "I think it will be more helpful if I remain objective." He stood there for a few awkward minutes and then said, "Have you fellows had anything to eat?"

"Not since seven," said Billy. "We'll break for lunch at one." He picked up his pencil and a yellow legal pad and started to write. He wrote four or five lines of dialogue, tore the page out, and handed it to me. "How about this?" he asked.

I read the dialogue and said, "It's funny, very funny," which it was.

Billy then handed the page to Sam. Sam read the lines and smiled. "What do you think?" asked Billy.

"I don't like to interfere with my writers until the script is finished," said Sam. He handed the page back to Billy and padded back to his room. Two hours later he returned. He was impeccably dressed in a blue blazer with brass buttons and white flannel trousers. He smelled like a French barber shop.

"I want you boys to come to lunch with me in Cannes," he said.

"No dice," said Billy. "We've got a lot of work to do and we'll blow the rest of the day if we chase off with you."

"How do I know you'll work if I leave you here?" asked Sam.

"You don't," said Billy. "You have to trust us. You're not paying us, so you have to trust us. Why do you want to go to Cannes?"

"To buy a yacht," said Sam.

Billy looked at Sam for a long moment. Then he looked at me and said, "Come on. This I must see."

*   *   *

We had lunch at the Hôtel du Cap with a yacht broker who showed us impressive photos of the motor yacht *Malahne,* a 198-foot dream boat that the Dutch owner had just had completely repainted, refurbished, and refitted with new radar. "Just like they have on U.S. aircraft carriers," said the broker. "The only kind of radar to have," said Billy.

When we finished lunch, the broker took us aboard the *Malahne.* Sam and I went on a tour with the broker, and Billy stayed on deck talking to some of the French crew. After a while he joined us, sidled up to Sam, and asked if he could have a word with him. He took Sam aside and said, "I've been talking to the crew. They tell me it takes nine people to run this boat and that's when it's in the harbor. When it's at sea, you'll need a crew of fourteen, day and night, twenty-four hours a day. Nobody can afford a boat this size anymore, Sam. You must be going crazy."

Sam looked at his friend patiently for a moment, then he said, "Don't be so plebeian, Billy."

Sam closed the deal for the *Malahne* ten days later, the same day Billy and I finished our rewrite of *Dangerous Silence.* Sam said he liked the script, and we waved goodbye to Billy as he took off for America from the Nice airport. Sam and I drove to the Hôtel du Cap for lunch. During lunch Sam told me more than I wanted to know about his plans for *Lawrence of Arabia.* He said he would sail the *Malahne* to the Jordanian port of Aqaba, where King Hussein would meet him and personally fly him around in the royal helicopter to scout locations. The more enthusiastic he became about the plans for *Lawrence of Arabia,* the slimmer the chances of making *Dangerous Silence* began to seem and the more I thought about what Willy Wyler had told me.

While we were having coffee I said, "Sam, are we going to make *Dangerous Silence?*"

He looked hurt for a few seconds, then said, "Of course we are, baby. What makes you ask such a question?"

"When?" I said.

"As soon as we do a little more work on the script," he said.

"I thought you liked it," I said. "You told Billy you liked it."

"I do, but it's not quite right yet."

"How's the script on *Lawrence of Arabia?*"

"Very good."

"Then you'll make that first, won't you?"

"Not necessarily."

"Why not?"

"Because the script's not quite right yet."

I smiled and shut up. Sam said, "Be patient, baby."

He sailed off to Jordan a week later. I didn't see him again for over a year.

When I returned to London, I met Willy Wyler at the White Elephant Club on Curzon Street. His first question was, "How's the picture going?" I think he smiled a little bit. I'm not sure.

I told him the whole story. Facts only. No exaggerations, no emotional outbursts, no self-pity, no recriminations.

"We said goodbye with a highball," I said. "Then we got high as a steeple. We were intelligent people. No tears, no fuss, hooray for us."

"How do you feel about Sam now?" said Willy.

"He might have been a headache, but he never was a bore," I said.

Willy smiled. I was sure this time. "Join the club," he said.

And that's what Kathie and I did. We joined the many ex–Hollywood residents who were in Europe in the late 'fifties and early 'sixties: John Huston, Deborah Kerr, Carl Foreman, David Niven, Charlie Chaplin, Joe Losey, Ava Gardner, Clark Gable, and several others, some who came and went. Some were blacklisted after the HUAC hearings, some were there for tax reasons, others were there just because they liked to work or live in Europe.

We didn't make a conscious decision to move to London. We went there on a job, to make *Dangerous Silence*. When the picture was canceled, we realized we had been living in London for over a year. Both children were in English schools, we were locked in to the lease on our Kensington flat for another eleven months, and we both loved the London life.

"I guess we live here now," said Kathie.

"Yes," I said, "I guess we do."

"I'll make the coffee," she said.

"Put a drop of Cointreau in mine."

Everyone Wants to Direct

flash-back/n. interruption of chronological sequence in a literary or theatrical work by in-
terjection of events of earlier occurrence

*A successful film director, like a successful president, em-
peror, general, or pirate, is sometimes idealistic in what he
seeks, but often cunning, deceitful, conniving, and scheming
in the way he pursues it, because the essence of his job is to
prevail over conflicting interests to promote his own interests, whether they be idealistic or opportunistic. He has to
create and manipulate constantly shifting emotions and alliances, first for one purpose and then another, maneuvering
the film, however indirectly, toward his vision of its future.*

I formed the above opinion by watching John Ford work,
working with him, and studying his films for a number of
years. He was a classic example of the successful film director
of his time, one of the last of a dying breed. I think the story of
the making of the two versions of the wartime "documentary"
(propaganda) film *December 7th* might give some insight into
his style, his character.

It also might reveal something about Gregg Toland, one of
Hollywood's best cameramen. Anyone who lists among his
credits *The Long Voyage Home, The Grapes of Wrath,* and
Citizen Kane had to be near, or at, the top. He was, in fact, a
great cameraman, but he had a flaw that he shared with some
other great cameramen, as well as with great and not-so-great

actors, film editors, writers, suit manufacturers, bankers, rich men, poor men, beggarmen, and thieves: Toland wanted to direct.

In 1939, more than twenty years before Sam Spiegel put me to work on *Dangerous Silence*, I was working in the cutting room on *The Grapes of Wrath* for John Ford. I had known Ford since I was nine years old, having worked for him as a child actor in *Mother Machree, The Informer*, and other movies and, later, as a film editor. In 1940 Ford formed an ad hoc, loosely disciplined U.S. Navy Reserve unit that he envisioned as a front-line photographic combat group should the United States become involved in the war. I enlisted and was sworn in as a second-class petty officer. Ford promised Toland that he would give him a picture to direct if Toland would enlist in his reserve unit and help train other enlistees in the fundamentals of photography. Toland enlisted and was sworn in as a lieutenant, junior grade.

The day after the Japanese attack on Pearl Harbor, Ford's unit was called to Washington and assigned to the Office of Strategic Services (OSS), a newly formed intelligence organization headed by Col. William ("Wild Bill") Donovan. Aside from combat photography, our job was to make films for internal OSS use (*How to Operate Behind Enemy Lines, German Industrial Manpower*, etc.). Other jobs were to make films for various government agencies and for the public.

In the period immediately following December 7, 1941, accurate information about foreign outposts was sketchy at best. Donovan ordered Ford to send camera teams to the Panama Canal Zone, Iceland, Murmansk, Honolulu, and other strategic places throughout the world and bring back photographic reports of current conditions. The uncensored film was then to be shown, at Donovan's discretion, to President Roosevelt, the joint chiefs of staff, and others.

Ford assigned Lt. Sam Engel to write and produce the Honolulu report. He assigned Gregg Toland to direct. (A promise kept, a dream realized.) A crew was selected, orders were cut, shots were given, equipment was chosen and packed, and off they went. Those left behind at the Field Photo Washington headquarters in the South Agriculture Building were disappointed to be kept out of the action. I know. I was one of them. I was originally assigned to the crew by Ford primarily because I was a film editor. He had wanted me to be on the scene when the film was shot, bring the first rushes back, do a quick edit job, and turn them over to Col. Donovan — a newsreellike operation. At the last minute, Toland persuaded Ford that he should be allowed to select his own crew, just as Ford did when *he* was directing. (Actually, Toland didn't want any Ford loyalists aboard.) Ford agreed and I unpacked.

A director's job (even a novice director's) is to prevail over conflicting interests in order to advance his own interests.

When no film arrived from Pearl Harbor after six weeks, Ford flew out to Honolulu. There he discovered that when you hand the ball (or camera) over to a frustrated director, he's liable to tuck it under his arm and run with it, which is exactly what Toland was doing. Just as he had seen Ford do many times, he got as far away from the "studio brass" — that is, the authority, in this case, Ford — as he could and was directing *his* movie, the one that *he* wanted to make. It turned out that he was not interested in newsreel work. He wanted to make a feature movie, with a story, proper actors, a political point of view (his), and so on.

When Ford arrived, Engel read him the script he was writing. Toland acted out some of the scenes he had shot and some that were still to be shot. He told Ford that Walter Huston, Harry Davenport, Dana Andrews, and some other Hollywood actors had agreed to act in some scenes to be shot at the Twentieth Century–Fox studio when he finished shooting in Honolulu. Ford was apprehensive about the idea of presenting a feature-length film with Hollywood actors and Toland's political philosophy to Donovan when what was wanted was a brief, factual report about what had happened at Pearl Harbor and who was to blame. He learned that Toland had little regard for military protocol and was stepping on a lot of toes in the sensitive post–December 7 era, and that some of the veteran Regular Navy officers (as opposed to wartime Reserves) were anxious to scuttle the Toland operation.

Ford arrived on a Sunday. On the following Monday, Toland was scheduled to shoot some scenes of the aftermath of the Japanese attack. Ford offered to go along and get some second-camera shots for Toland. While Ford was shooting, a U.S. Navy station wagon pulled up. A two-star admiral and three other high-ranking officers piled out. They were introduced to Ford and said they had come to watch the filming. Movie sets, like circuses and traffic accidents, always attract crowds, even during a war.

Ford directed a scene, and when he said, "OK, cut," the admiral said, "Wouldn't it be better if the seaman saluted before he hands the captain his bag instead of after?" Lt. Comdr. Ford looked at him for a few seconds, then he looked at his two stars, and then he said, "Yes, sir. Let's do it again." He made the shot again the admiral's way and moved on to his next setup. The visitors followed.

By this time, the admiral had been bitten and infected by what was known in the industry as the "Wouldn't it be better if . . ." bug. This bug usually bites only directors manqué and is also sometimes called the "Anyone can direct" bug or "The horse's ass" bug. The person bitten is commonly known as an "iffer" or "second guesser" or "Monday-morning quarterback."

As a veteran Hollywood professional, Ford could recognize an "iffer" from a mile away, even without his glasses, and after long and successful practice with New York bankers, studio heads, movie stars, producers, foreign and domestic diplomats, and Shirley Temple's mother, he knew how to handle them. He politely respected the first "wouldn't it be better if . . ." and waited for the inevitable second. In this case, he listened while the admiral explained an intricate camera move that he felt sure would give the next shot more "punch." Ford was noted for making some of the best films ever made and seldom moving the camera. When the admiral finished, Ford stared out at the harbor and what was left of the U.S. Pacific Fleet. He then slowly lit his pipe and turned to the admiral.

"Sir," he said, "do you ever direct complete movies, or do you just kibitz when you have nothing better to do?" He turned his back on the admiral and walked over to Jack McKenzie, his cameraman. "Put the camera on a tripod and set it up here," he said. "Let's stop wasting time. We've got a lot of work to do today."

The next day Ford was given urgent orders from the admiral's office to leave Pearl Harbor. Before he left, he warned Toland and Engel to be careful, to "be inky," and not to let anyone know what they were doing, but when he saw them exchange glances, he suspected that his warnings were falling on deaf ears. And when Engel winked at Toland and rolled his eyes, Ford was convinced of his suspicions. He saluted and said to his two lieutenants, "You're doing a fine job, lads. Keep up the good work." Then he sailed away on the U.S.S. *Salt Lake City* to another theater of operations, far away from Toland and his first directing job.

A successful film director (especially a veteran) is often cunning, deceitful, conniving, and scheming.

The U.S.S. *Salt Lake City* was involved in Col. Jimmy Doolittle's raid on the Japanese home islands. Ford was aboard. After that, the OSS broke the Japanese code and discovered that the Japanese were planning a major naval and air attack on Midway Island in June 1942. Ford persuaded Col. Donovan to send him and Jack McKenzie to Midway to photograph the action.

There the Japanese lost their first-line carrier strength and most of their best-trained naval pilots, bringing some kind of parity to the Pacific. The Japanese canceled their plans for the invasion of New Caledonia, Fiji, and Samoa, and they lost all but the last vestiges of their earlier strategic initiative.

Ford had personally photographed the action at Midway. He brought four hours of 16-mm color film back and assigned me to edit it, under his supervision, to eighteen minutes. In July 1942, I picked up the first composite print of what came to be titled *The Battle of Midway* at the Technicolor lab in Hollywood. I phoned Ford in Washington and requested my orders. He said, "Take it to Twentieth Century–Fox studio and show it to Lt. Toland and Lt. Engel. They're still working on the *December 7th* picture there. Run it for *them* alone. Don't let anyone else in the projection room. Phone me after the running and tell me their comments."

During the first 75 percent of the running, no one spoke. Toward the end, where the American casualties are being buried at sea and "My Country 'Tis of Thee" is heard in the distance, Lt. Engel jumped up and said, "The sonofabitch stole our scenes! That's exactly what we have in our picture, the stuff we told him about in Pearl Harbor!" Toland sat slumped in his seat.

When the picture was finished, the lights went up and I could see that Toland's face was whiter than usual. As the two officers walked out, I heard Engel say, "Don't you see what's happened? The bastard has sabotaged our picture! Everything we've been working on for six months!" The soundproof door closed and I was alone. If Toland said anything, I didn't hear it. He certainly didn't say anything to me. Neither of them said a word to me before, during, or after the running, not even hello or goodbye.

Ford phoned me that night and asked for a report on the running. I said, "Engel seemed angry and Toland seemed sick." Ford said, "I don't want your editorial comments; I just want to know what they said."

"Neither of them said anything to me."

"Did they say anything to each other?"

"Toland didn't say anything, and Engel said, 'The sonofabitch stole our scenes.' "

"Is that all he said?"

"No. He also said, 'The bastard has sabotaged our picture.' "

"Maybe he's right," said Ford. "Bring the print to me in Washington as soon as you can get on a plane."

Walter Wanger was a producer with class. He was well educated, well spoken, well dressed, and, well, he was the president of the Academy of Motion Picture Arts and Sciences, thus a very important man in Hollywood. He had produced *Stagecoach* and Eugene O'Neill's *The Long Voyage Home* with Ford. They knew each other well.

Two weeks after I returned to Washington, Ford called me to his office, introduced me to Wanger, and asked me to show him *The Battle of Midway*. When the picture finished, Wanger said, "It's magnificent. Where's Jack? I want to talk to him." The lights went up and Ford was sitting in the back of the projection room. He had sneaked in sometime during the running.

"What do you think?" he said to Wanger.

"It's definitely award material, Jack. It's wonderful."

"Oh, for Christ's sakes, Walter," said Ford. "I'm not interested in awards. I just want to remind you Hollywood guys
that somebody's out there fighting a war."

Wanger winced slightly, but he kept his dignity. "The scene
of the burial at sea reminds me of our scene in *The Long
Voyage Home*," he said. Ford was lighting his pipe, a thing he
spent a lot of time doing. He froze and looked right into Wanger's eyes for a long time. Wanger looked back. Then he said,
"I've seen some damned good documentaries in the past
weeks, but *The Battle of Midway* is the only one in color. It's
beautiful. With so many good films, the Academy's going to
have a difficult time making a choice."

Ford finished lighting his pipe, puffed a few times, and then
said, "Why can't you have more than one award?"

In 1942, and in that year only, there were four documentary
awards given by the Academy: *The Battle of Midway* —
U.S. Navy, Twentieth Century–Fox; *Kokoda Front Line* —
Australian News Information Bureau; *Moscow Strikes Back*
— Artkino (Russian); *Prelude to War* — U.S. Army Special
Reserve Services.

Toland and Engel finally finished their feature picture *December 7th* and showed it to the Navy Department. The navy
reacted by confiscating the print and ordering Ford to lock up
the negative. Toland went into a deep depression and requested duty as far away from Washington as possible. Ford
sent him to Rio de Janeiro to set up a Field Photo Branch
there.

Later, the Navy Department requested the Field Photo
Branch of the Office of Strategic Services to make a short "documentary" (propaganda) film for the Navy Industrial Incentive Program. Ford assigned me to the project and told me to
run the Toland-Engel *December 7th* film and tell him what I
thought of it. I told him that I thought the Navy Department
had been right, that it should go back in the vault. He said he
wasn't interested in smart-aleck remarks from enlisted men,

that it was a beautiful picture, that Lt. Toland was a great cameraman and a fine director, and did I think it could be made into an Industrial Incentive film? I said I thought it could.

He said, "Fine. Go to work on it. Remember, if anyone asks you what you are working on, always say you're working on something else."

He assigned Budd Schulberg to write some new narration, and I cut the eighty-three minutes down to thirty-four. When I finished, there were 4,410 feet (forty-nine minutes) of Hollywood actors and political philosophy on the cutting-room floor. What was left was film of the actual Japanese attack on Pearl Harbor and an upbeat ending of American workers rebuilding the United States fleet.

"You remember Mr. Wanger, Bob," said Lt. Comdr. Ford. "He's the president of the Academy of Motion Picture Arts and Sciences."

Wanger and I shook hands. "Good to see you again, Mr. Wanger," I said.

"Walter wants to look at Toland's film," said Ford. He turned to Wanger. "*December 7th* is not for the general public," he said. "In fact, some of the scenes are restricted unless you have a clearance. We may be in trouble if we show it to a civilian."

"Then why did you invite me down from New York to see it?" said Wanger.

"Because I want you to see Gregg's directorial work. He's done a fine job and I think he deserves some credit. I want to show it to as many civilians as possible."

After Wanger saw the film he said to me, "Stunning. I think it must be shown to the Academy." We went back to Ford's office and Wanger said, "You're right, Jack. Gregg did a great job. I'm glad he used your burial at sea from *The Battle of Midway*. It works perfectly."

"It's Eugene O'Neill's burial at sea," said Ford.

The Industrial Incentive version of *December 7th* by the U.S. Navy, Field Photographic Branch, Office of Strategic Services, won the Academy Award for Best Documentary (Short

Subjects) for 1943. I'm not sure that Toland or Engel ever saw this version.

A successful director has to create and manipulate constantly shifting emotions and alliances, first for one purpose and then another, maneuvering the film, however indirectly, toward his version of its future.

From *World Press Review*, September 1984, "The Shah's Son":

> Reza Ciro Pahlavi, the twenty-three-year-old son of the late Shah of Iran, lives in luxury in Rabat, Morocco, waiting for a chance to go home and assume his father's throne. . . . "He lives under the threat of death — as do all the Pahlavis — proclaimed by the Khomeini regime." . . .
>
> He says he offered to serve in the army in Iran's war against Iraq but the army did not even answer. If he cannot regain his throne, he says, he would like to become a movie director.

Never Trust a Film Editor

pro-pa-gan-da/n. ideas, facts, or allegations
spread deliberately to further one's cause or to
damage an opposing cause

Ford assigned me to make a film about the National Gallery
of Art in Washington, D.C. The gallery had opened in 1941
and was considered one of the wonders of the art world, but I
didn't see what that had to do with the war effort, especially
when there were rumors of an imminent invasion of the European continent. I asked Ford what kind of picture he had in
mind; did he want a propaganda picture?

He looked at me a long time, looked away, and looked back
at me. Finally he said, "How do you spell that word?" I
spelled it for him and he said, "Don't ever let me hear you use
that word again in my presence as long as you are under my
command."

I saluted and said, "Yessir." I had been saying "Yessir" to
him for seventeen years, so I figured one more wouldn't hurt,
especially when he was a lieutenant commander and I was a
second-class petty officer.

"And don't salute unless you have a hat on," Ford said.

I said, "Yessir," again.

"We will eventually invade the continent," said Ford.
"Gen. Donovan and the State Department have decided that,
after the initial assault, the Allied forces will have to dig in
and prepare for the advance into Holland, Italy, France, or
wherever the assault takes place. We will have to deal with

the local population from a public-relations point of view. Americans are not necessarily loved by everyone in the world."

No, I guess not, I thought. Especially after we've subjected them to penetration bombing for several months.

"I think the invasion will probably be somewhere along the French coast," said Ford. "The French are cultured people, even the peasants. We don't want them to think we're barbarians, do we?"

"No sir, I guess not," I asskissed.

"So the idea is to make a short picture that has nothing to do with the war and issue sixteen-millimeter prints and projectors to all combat units, and they can show the movie to the locals wherever they happen to be billeted."

I tried to picture some GI's rounding up a bunch of war-weary French peasants and showing them a movie about an art gallery, and I wondered if it would prove that we were not barbarians.

"Get over to the National Gallery the first thing in the morning, look it over, and report back to me tomorrow afternoon. Lt. Arling will be your cameraman. He's very good with color. He was trained at Technicolor."

I knew Arling. He was a first-rate cameraman. "Who's the boss?" I said.

"You know there's no boss in this organization," said Ford. "Except me."

"I mean, who's in charge of this art gallery project?"

Ford said, "What's your rank?"

I said, "Petty officer, second class." Ford didn't say anything, so I said, "Sir."

"What's Arling's rank?"

"He's a full lieutenant, sir."

"Any more questions?" said Ford.

The National Gallery of Art is housed in a beautiful building. In 1942 they were having the most comprehensive exhibition of French Impressionist paintings ever shown in America. In the early days of the war, before the Nazis had occupied Paris, some of the finest paintings from the Louvre and other museums, as well as from private collections, had been sent to America for safekeeping. Great works, starting with Bonnard and going all the way down the alphabet to Vuillard, were represented. When Lt. Arling and I were shown just a sample of the vast collection, I thought Arling would have a stroke. He wanted to shoot thousands of feet of color film of every painting in the building. I pointed out that we would wind up with a forty-hour movie to show to the French peasants, and he said, "Give me a better idea."

I had been to the basement and seen the new, unique air-conditioning unit. It was all shiny-grey, black and white and dark grey, and looked like a futuristic movie set. I led Arling down and showed it to him. "Why don't we start here?" I said.

"It's extraordinary, but it's all black and white and grey," he answered.

"Exactly."

"My specialty is color."

"Of course it is, but that will come later, after you have made some of the most beautiful abstract black-and-white shots since *Citizen Kane*. The contrast when we go upstairs and burst into color for the second half of the movie will be sensational."

He finally agreed, and that's the way we shot the picture. I edited it, put Chopin's "Revolutionary Étude" over the black-and-white "revolutionary" air-conditioning unit and Debussy's "Prélude à l'après-midi d'un faune" and other "colorful" piano compositions over the explosion of color upstairs. The effect was quite stunning. Of all the great paintings at our disposal, we featured "Man Spreading Manure," "Woman Feeding Child," and other works by Jean-François Millet because he had been born in the hamlet of Gruchy, on the west coast of France, where Ford expected the invasion to take place.

Lt. Arling and I showed the twenty-minute film to Comdr. Ford, he showed it to Col. Donovan, and Donovan showed it to anyone in Washington that he could get to sit still for twenty minutes. Everyone was delighted. The Field Photo Branch of the OSS, a *combat* unit, had made a "lyrical, artistic film"!

"If that doesn't show the French peasants that Americans are cultured, nothing will," said Donovan. A print was rushed to the OSS headquarters in London with instructions to show it to Gen. Eisenhower.

A few days later, Ford read a coded cable to me and

Lt. Arling: MAN SPREADING EXCELLENT MANURE. CONGRATULATIONS. GALLIC NEXT OSSLON. When decoded it read: "National Gallery film excellent. Showing to de Gaulle and Malraux OSS London."

Ford shook our hands and said, "Well done, lads." A week later Ford was promoted to full commander, Arling was given a Letter of Commendation, and I was promoted to petty officer, first class.

And that was all I heard of the National Gallery of Art film until three weeks later, when Ford called me into his office. Lt. Arling was away on leave. This was the first time I had seen Ford since my promotion. He handed me a long, coded message that started, URGENT MAN SPREADING MANURE . . . I turned to the next page, which was the decoded version.

"Read it aloud," said Ford.

I started to read: "French outraged by National Gallery . . ."

I stopped reading. The next word was *propaganda,* and I remembered Ford's order about not mentioning the word as long as I was under his command. I didn't know where else to look, so I looked at Ford's feet. He was wearing dirty tennis shoes with his navy blue commander's uniform. "Go on," he said.

"It's a word I've been ordered not to say, sir."

"Start over and say it anyway."

I said, "Yessir," and started to read again: "French outraged by National Gallery propaganda film. Their opinion if shown to French peasants same would throw rocks at screen and scream 'Barbarian Americans have stolen French masterpieces.' Urgent you lock up all copies and throw away key until after war. London copy already destroyed. OSS London."

At the bottom in someone's handwriting was scribbled, "Chopin was Polish, not French. His father was French."

Ford didn't usually show his emotions, but I could tell he was sad. "I see you have an extra stripe," he said.

"Yessir," I answered.

"You earned it," he said. "What are you working on?"

"The recruiting film for the SPARS."

"What the hell is that?"

"The women's Coast Guard."

"Well, stop what you're doing, round up every scrap of material connected with the National Gallery of Art film, lock it up in the vault, and bring me the key."

"Yessir," I said. I started to leave and Ford said, "Did you think you were making a propaganda film?"

"Sort of," I said.

"Well, you weren't," said Ford. "You made an honest film and you should be proud of it."

"Yessir," I said.

A short time later, Comdr. Ford invited me to his private projection room and said he wanted to show me a German film that one of our field men had brought in from Portugal.

The film opens with the title *America the Beautiful*. The song of the same title is being sung by Bing Crosby on the sound track:

> *Oh beautiful for spacious skies,*
> *For amber waves of grain,*

On the screen are newsreel scenes of violent attacks on defenseless blacks by club-wielding policemen during the Detroit race riots in the 'thirties. After one slow-motion close shot of a black head being split open, there is a close-up of President Roosevelt laughing heartily. Bing sings on:

> *For purple mountain majesties*

Then come newsreel scenes of women wrestling in a boxing ring filled with mud, and other women wrestling in a ring filled with dead fish. Intercut with these shots are close-ups of Mrs. Roosevelt, dressed for the opera, smiling and applauding politely.

> *Above the fruited plain!*

The last scene is a newsreel shot of the Roosevelt family gathered around a table at Hyde Park for their annual Thanksgiving dinner. As Roosevelt reaches out to carve the turkey, the camera cuts to a close-up of the turkey, which dissolves to a close-up of a global map of the world. The knife comes in and slices off the Scandinavian countries and puts them on a plate, which Roosevelt hands offstage. The camera pans

up from the plate to a smiling close-up of Prime Minister
Winston Churchill.

> *America! America!*
> *God shed his grace on thee*

Cut back to the globe. Camera follows as President
Roosevelt slices off Italy, puts it on a plate, and holds it out to a
dour-looking General de Gaulle. De Gaulle nods and salutes
President Roosevelt.

Cut to close-up of President Roosevelt. He puts a cigarette
in a long holder in his mouth at a jaunty angle and smiles
happily.

> *And crown thy good with brotherhood*
> *From sea to shining sea!*

The scene fades out.

The projection room was pitch-dark. Ford struck a match
and lit his pipe. When it was well lit, he puffed a few times,
turned his shadowy head to me, and said, *"That's* a propaganda picture." He got up and walked out, leaving me in
the dark room.

5

It's All Laid On

Col. Donovan sent Comdr. Ford to London to set up an OSS Field Photo office. At that time, Britain was primarily concerned with Adolf Hitler. Quite rightly, too. The Germans were bombing London, Manchester, and Liverpool regularly and theatening to invade the "tight little island" at the earliest opportunity.

The Americans were more concerned with the Japanese. After the attack on Pearl Harbor on December 7, 1941, the United States forces reorganized and fought uphill battles in the Pacific until their victory over the Japanese fleet at Midway Island in June 1942. If any one action can be called the turning point of the war in the Pacific, it is probably the battle of Midway. For the Allies it was a great strategic victory. Ford wanted to show our documentary film *The Battle of Midway* to the British to prove that we were actually in the war with them.

A coded cable arrived at the OSS Field Photo office in Washington: SEND PROPAGANDA EDITOR MIDWAY PRINT URGENT OSSLON. Decoded, it read: "Send Parrish to London with print of *The Battle of Midway* urgent."

The OSS outfitted me with a civilian suit, a nonmilitary passport, and a specially made suitcase with a secret compartment for the two reels of 35-mm inflammable nitrate film. At dawn on September 16, 1942, I boarded an American Export Airlines flying boat in New York with twenty-two other military personnel, all pretending to be civilians so that we could land in neutral Ireland before proceeding to London.

My OSS briefing officer had given me explicit instructions on how to handle myself if anyone questioned me. "Lie," he said. "Say you're in Ireland on a fishing trip or to visit your mother's grave or something. You'll only be there a few hours and then an RAF plane will take you to London."

"I thought no military planes from belligerent countries were supposed to land in neutral countries," I said. "Won't the Irish be angry when they find out about this planeload of liars?"

"They don't have to find out," he said. "They already know. They've been briefed the same as you're being briefed. It's all fixed. It's arranged. It's laid on. All you have to do is lie. Christ, you can lie, can't you?"

"Oh, sure," I said. "I can lie. That's no problem. I do it all the time. The only trouble is that when I blurt out a bald-faced lie, the kind I learned in OSS training school, my face turns purple and I bat my eyes and stutter. This sometimes causes my interrogator to say, 'You're full of shit,' and when he says that, I cry."

"You cry?" said my briefing officer.

"Yes," I said. "I burst into tears. I don't know why, but that's what I do."

"Does your commanding officer know about this?" he said.

"Yes," I said. "He's Irish. The Irish cry a lot too. My commanding officer says it's good for the soul."

The briefing officer was quiet for a minute. He looked out of his window at the beautiful fall colors of 25th and E Street NW, Washington, D.C., then he bit his bottom lip and looked over at me out of the corner of his eye. He didn't move his head. Our eyes met for a few pregnant seconds and he said, "OK, let's go over it again. One: you're a petty officer in the navy assigned to the Field Photograph Branch of the Office of Strategic Services. Two: you're traveling to London via neutral Ireland as a civilian. Three: you're carrying a two-reel propaganda film, *The Battle of Midway*, to Comdr. John Ford, the chief of the Field Photographic Branch of the OSS. Four: the film is classified secret. Five: you cry if someone says you're full of shit. Six: you —"

"Just a minute," I said. "You left out the lying. That's important. That's what makes someone say I'm full of shit and that's when I cry."

"OK," said the briefing officer. "You lie, the guy says you're full of shit, and you cry. OK?"

"Yes, sir," I said.

"Well, if you should reach that stage in your OSS career in Ireland, give your interrogator this paper."

He handed me a paper with two names on it: The Hon. Lord Grey, U.S. ambassador to Ireland, and Richard Watts, an American journalist stationed in Dublin. "Tell your interrogator to contact either of these people," he said. "They'll know what to do."

"Right," I said, and stood to attention, heels together, toes 45 degrees, eyes straight ahead.

"Relax," said the briefing officer. "I'm a civilian." He handed me a manila envelope full of papers and said, "And you are too, until you get to London." He shook my hand and said, "Don't worry about it. It's all laid on."

We landed at Botwood, Newfoundland, and while the plane was being refueled, I bought some oranges in the U.S. Army PX. Fourteen hours later we descended through fluffy white clouds, and there below us was the west coast of Ireland, green as could be. The sparkling fields were separated by stone fences, and the mouth of the River Shannon, where we were to land, was calm and soft and inviting. The big flying boat settled down like a duck coming home after a hard winter, and a short time later we were on a bus on the way to Shannon, where the RAF plane was to pick us up. A fine, misty rain started and some of the other passengers made jokes about the *soft* Irish weather.

This was my first trip abroad and the first time I had been exposed to the strange phenomenon of Americans breaking into a kind of cornball dialect as soon as they leave United States territorial waters. "Shurre and it's a bit of soft weather we're havin'," said a United States Navy admiral who was enroute to London to help plan the invasion of Europe. "Aye, that it is," said an air force general. In their civilian suits they both looked like salesmen from Macy's. From time to time the

sun would pop out and the countryside would become so brilliant and clear that one could hardly bear it. Then the mist and
rain would start again and make the countryside look dour and
depressing, and one could hardly bear that either. Each
change was noted with some corny half-Irish comment by one
of my high-ranking fellow passengers, and their comments
were the most unbearable thing of all.

The Irish official at Shannon looked at our phony passports
and passed all of the passengers along to a waiting plane,
except me. He asked me to step over into another room and
wait for him. Then, through a small window, I watched him
walk out to the plane, give the passports to a steward, and
stand in the rain while the plane taxied and took off. I had
been half kidding when I told my OSS briefing officer that I
cried, but when that RAF Dakota, pretending to be a civilian
air-transport plane, took off for London, I almost burst into
tears.

I looked around and saw that there were three objects in the
room: two straight chairs and the large leather bag that the
OSS had given me. The seal on the lock had not been broken,
so I assumed the Irish officials had not discovered the two-reel
propaganda film in the hidden compartment. Then I began to
think, what if they had discovered it? What difference would it
make? The Battle of Midway had taken place months before.
The Irish probably didn't care then and they probably didn't
care now.

While I was trying to figure out why I had been singled out
for special treatment, the door opened and three small,
barefoot boys came in. They stood in the corner of the room
and stared at me for a while, then one of them said something
in Gaelic. I couldn't understand him, so I did what American
GI's usually did under the circumstances: I offered them some
chewing gum. They accepted it eagerly and grinned and
spoke Gaelic to each other. I found the oranges left over from
the Botwood stopover in my knapsack and offered them to the
three boys. They were curious, but they wouldn't actually
touch the oranges. I put them on one of the chairs, and the
boys circled around them as though they were adders. After a
while, I picked up one of the oranges, threw it in the air with
my right hand, bounced it off my left elbow, and finally caught

it behind my back with my right hand. This was a trick I had learned when I was a substitute pitcher on the Fairfax High School baseball team in Los Angeles. The boys seemed to like my little act, so I performed it, with variations, until the immigration officer came in. This time he had another uniformed man with him, a brute whom I cast as the fingernail puller. I made a final, sensational catch without even looking at the orange and turned and faced my enemies.

"Is this your passport?"

"Yes." Pause. "Sir."

He pointed to my bag. "Is this your bag?"

"Yes, sir."

"Are you a member of the armed forces of any country engaged in hostilities with any other country?"

I could feel the "You're full of shit" coming up with a genuine Irish accent, not like the phonies on the plane, and I didn't want my three new barefoot friends with running noses to see me crying, so I said, "I've been trying to get these chaps to accept some oranges from Botwood, Newfoundland, but they seem reluctant to accept them."

"They've never seen an orange," said the fingernail puller.

"Well," I said, "I wonder if you would explain to them what an orange is and tell them that there's one for each of them." He spoke some Gaelic to the three boys, gave them each an orange, and herded them out of the room.

The other officer stood by patiently, and when the boys had left he said, "Won't you sit down?" I did, relieved that he seemed to have forgotten his line of interrogation. He hadn't, of course, and when he repeated his question about armed forces and hostilities, I felt the blood rush to my head and my eyes began to flutter. I tried to answer "No" or "Yes" or "I don't think so," but I couldn't get any words past my teeth, so I just shook my head.

"I have reason to believe that you are carrying photographic equipment in that bag," he said. "I must ask you to open it for inspection."

I didn't consider my film "photographic equipment." The blood left my head and went back where it belonged. My eyes stopped batting and I said in a loud, clear, unstuttery voice, "Here is the key, sir."

He motioned to the fingernail puller, who opened the bag and dumped all of my personal belongings on the floor. He then closed the bag and tried to set it upright. It toppled over. He tried again with the same result. The weight of the two rolls of 35-mm color film in the false compartment on one side of the bag toppled it over each time he put it upright.

The first officer said, "Please wait here." He then said something in Gaelic to the fingernail puller, who picked up the bag and followed the first officer out of the room, leaving me and my belongings and the two chairs.

After two hours, the fingernail puller came back with my bag and the three barefoot boys. (They turned out to be his sons.) He said I would have to remain in Shannon until the London plane came in the next day, that there was no photographic equipment in my bag, only some rolls of celluloid, and that there was no accommodation for me, but that I could sleep at his house, which was only a short way from the airport. His sons would take my bag to the house and he and I could stop at the Shamrock pub for a wee drop. When we got home his missus would have a fine meal waiting for us. He said something in Gaelic to the boys and they packed the bag and left.

I thought about giving the fingernail puller my letter to the ambassador and Richard Watts, but he was beginning to seem like a nice guy and hadn't even looked at my fingernails, so I said, "Can we get into the Shamrock now?" He admitted that we could, and after quite a few Irish whiskeys I said, "Why me?"

"Why you what?" he said.

"Why did you pick me out?" I said. "Who gave you the tip about the photographic equipment?"

"Oh," he said. "That. It came from Galway. The O'Fearna family there has an American relative named John Ford. He passed the word along to detain a certain Robert Parrish, but to keep him only for a few hours and not to harm him. So you see now, that's what we've done. You've been detained but not harmed. My Maggie will fix you a fine meal, and you'll be in London tomorrow night, more's the pity."

The meal was excellent. Maggie was pink-cheeked and soft and would never have let her husband pull out my fingernails, even if he had wanted to. She had four other children, not counting the orange boys. Three were girls and the fourth was another boy, aged two months, who nursed on his mother's beautiful white breast while we ate dinner.

"Why did John Ford want me detained in Ireland?" I said.

"Ah, well," said Patrick, the now non–fingernail puller. "We don't know that, now, do we?"

"No, I guess we don't," I said. "But it seems a strange thing for my commanding officer to do."

"Not strange a'tall," said Patrick. "He can't be your commanding officer if you're not in the military service, now can he?"

"Well, no, not if you look at it that way," I said.

"Well, there you are," said Patrick. "Now let's forget about all this and you come in and teach the boys how to bounce the oranges on their elbows."

6

Welcome to Britain

I presented my orders to the duty officer at the U.S. Navy headquarters at 18 Grosvenor Square in London and was assigned a billet in a private residence around the corner, at 87 Green Street. Some of the houses in the area had been bombed, but No. 87 was in reasonably good shape. Blackout curtains had been fitted on the windows and the electricity and water worked, except on the top floor. Rooms in the house had been assigned to U.S. Navy personnel according to rank. Officers occupied the ground floor and the next three. A group of chief petty officers from the PX had established themselves in hedonistic luxury in the subbasement. As the newest and lowest ranked enlisted man, I was told to keep climbing until I came to a door that was too low to walk through.

"That will be the tweeny's room," said the billeting chief. "You can bunk there tonight with the three marines who came in this morning. We haven't got the blackout curtains up yet, so don't turn on any lights. Have you got a helmet?"

"Yes, sir," I said.

"You haven't got two helmets, have you?"

I tried to think up some joke about how only two-headed sailors needed two helmets but thought better of it when I saw the four red hash-marks on the CPO's sleeve. Each mark meant four years' service in the Regular Navy. The sign on his desk read GROTSKY, B.J., CPO, USN.

"No, sir," I said. "Are you supposed to have two?"

"Depends on whether you want to pee and wash out of the same helmet," he said. "There's no water on the top floor at Number Eighty-seven, so if you want to wash, you have to fill your helmet in the basement and carry it up. Then if you want to pee, you have to empty the helmet, pee in it, and the next morning carry it down to the toilet on the first floor. If you had two helmets, you could save yourself a lot of climbing."

"Yes, sir, I guess I could," I said, "But unfortunately I've only got this one helmet." I showed it to him. "Why couldn't I just walk down to the first floor and pee in the toilet and save the helmet for air raids?"

The bosun's mate looked at me for what seemed like a long time and then said quietly, "OK, Mac, do it your way." He cleaned the sleepy-seeds from the corners of his eyes and then said, "And cut out the 'sir' shit. I'm a chief petty officer."

He got a billeting form out of a drawer and I said, "What's a tweeny?"

"What's a what?" he said.

"A tweeny," I said. "You said I would be in the tweeny's room with three marines."

"A tweeny is what the Limeys call an upstairs maid," he said.

"Oh," I said.

He looked at my orders and said, "Another OSS guy. Oh So Special. You know you guys are a pain in the ass, don't you?"

"Yes, I guess we are," I said.

"What in the hell are you doing over here anyway?" he said.

"Just following orders," I said. "You know how it is in the navy."

"No, Mac. How is it?" he said.

"Well, now, take tonight," I said. "I didn't ask to be sent to England and you probably didn't either. Yet, here we are, two Americans, both in London, both doing our jobs. You're probably used to it by now, but it's my first trip abroad. I find it all very interesting."

"Shee-it," he said and started to fill out my billeting form.

"Won't it be rather crowded?" I said.

"Won't what be crowded?" he said, not looking up.

"The room at the top of Number Eighty-seven Green Street," I said. "I mean, with three marines and me and a tweeny and all those helmets. If it's a room that's not big enough for me to walk into in the first place, what's it going to be like with four men and one tweeny, all washing and peeing in the dark?"

He handed me my billeting slip and said, "Look, Mac, I hate to break this to you on your first night in London, when everything is so interesting and all, but there won't actually *be* a tweeny in the room. That's just what they call it, a tweeny's room. There'll just be you and three marines. I checked them in earlier. They're nice chaps. You'll like 'em. Just came back from Guadalcanal. Now take your gear, turn right on North Audley Street, left on Green Street, and keep walking until you come to Number Eighty-seven."

I almost said "Yes, sir," but some inner voice whispered, "He hates to be called 'sir,' stupid," so I pointed the forefinger of my right hand at him as though it were a pistol. Then I bent my right thumb as though it were a trigger or the hammer of the pistol; I don't know which. I hate firearms. I clicked my teeth like a fellow trying to remove a corn husk from between a molar and another molar, and I winked an eye and said, "Right, chief."

He studied me for a brief moment and then said, "The OSS office is at Seventy-two Grosvenor Street. Report there tomorrow morning. The navy mess is in the basement at Sixty-two Green Street." He picked up a copy of *Stars and Stripes* and started to read.

"OK, chief," I said. "Thanks for everything." He didn't answer, so I said, "Do you mind if I ask you a question, chief?" He looked up, but he still didn't answer. "Why do they call them tweenies?" I said.

He put the paper down, then leaned forward deliberately and said, "Because they're Limeys, you OSS asshole. Now fuck off."

By the time I had moled my way to the top floor at No. 87 with my seabag, my eyes were used to the dark but my legs were ready to cave in. I stopped on the landing of the fifth floor, where the narrow stairs ended, and took a deep breath. Muffled sounds came from behind a small door. I walked over (I guess you could say I tiptoed over) and listened to the voices of three Americans. One had a flat, nasal, Arkansas hill-country twang and the other two probably came from around New York, maybe New Jersey.

"Shepherd's Market," said one of the New York/New Jersey voices. "That's the place for pussy."

"Maybe," said the southerner.

"That's what the chief said. He said there's bags of pussy in Shepherd's Market if you wanta pay for it. He said they even got some French pussy, but you gotta pay for it."

"What's wrong with paying for it?"

"Nothin's wrong with payin' for it, if you got the money."

"We got the money. We got our combat pay."

"I'm against payin' for it."

"That's because you're cheap and would rather pull your pud. Gimme the shoe polish."

"Whattaya polishing ya shoes for? They ain't gonna look at your shoes, not unless ya wear 'em on the end of your joint."

"He said the French girls were better'n the Belgian girls, but they cost more."

"I think he's fulla shit. I don't think he knows his ass from a hot rock."

"Maybe not, but maybe he knows a piece of French ass from a hot rock. Where did he say Shepherd's Market is?"

"On Curzon Street, right across from the Christian Science Church. Let's go, before they run outa pussy."

Footsteps started toward the door. I didn't want to get caught eavesdropping on this delicate conversation, so I quickly shouldered my seabag and knocked on the door. The footsteps stopped, but I could feel the presence of the three marines through the door. In the distance the low wail of an air-raid siren started. "Who izzit?" said one of the N.Y/N.J. voices.

"Chief Grotsky sent me," I said.

"Who the fuck is he?" said the other N.Y./N.J. voice.

"He's the billeting chief," I said. "He says I'm to stay here tonight."

Silence, then a whisper from the southerner. "Grotsky's the swabbie who told us about the pussy market."

One of the others grunted and said, "You better be a fuckin' midget if you expect to stay in here," and he opened the door.

In the dim light I could see that two of the marines were much bigger than I was. The third, the southerner, was a bit shorter, but he was wide and tough and as foul-mouthed as the other two. All three were lean and mean and trim and polished. There wasn't an ounce of fat on any of them except in their close-cropped heads. They smelled of Blitz, Kiwi, Listerine, and Vitalis. They were in their dress uniforms, and each wore a campaign ribbon from Guadalcanal (red, white, and blue stripes on an orange background) with two battle stars.

The two northerners were privates, first class: single stripers. The third, the southerner, was a corporal: two stripes. If the truth were known, I outranked all of them, but fortunately the truth was not known. As far as the three marines could see, I was a plain sailor, with a pea jacket, a flat blue crumpled pancake hat, a twenty-four-hour growth of beard, and no combat ribbons. I wasn't lean and mean and horny, and I was exhausted from my trip across the Atlantic and my climb up the stairs with my seabag.

"Hi," I said.

"This room is full, sailor," said the corporal. "The chief musta made a mistake."

I took the billeting chit out of my pocket and looked at it. "Eighty-seven Green Street, fifth floor," I said.

The corporal said, "Lemme see that." I showed it to him and he said, "We only got three beds in here."

I tried to look into the room, but the three bodies blocked the view. "I don't mind sharing," I said.

The corporal glanced around at his two companions and said, "We don't go in for that kinda shit in the Marine Corps, sailor."

I dropped my seabag to the floor and said, "What kinda shit did you have in mind, corporal?"

"Sharing beds shit," he said. "That's what kinda shit. We ain't at sea now, and we ain't fags, and we don't bugger sailors."

I sat down on my seabag. "Thank you for pointing that out to me," I said. "Don't worry about it, I'll sleep out here in the hall." In the distance the first air-raid siren had been joined by three or four others, closer than the first one. Together they made an undulating, mournful, unworldly sound.

"Why can't he sleep on the cot?" said one of the tall marines.

"Because we're gonna bring home some French pussy and we gotta have a place to put it, that's why," said the corporal.

"They got their own rooms, Lamar," said the tallest marine. "That's part of what ya pay for. Let 'im use the cot."

The corporal handed me back my billeting ticket and said, "OK, sailor. You can stay for this one night."

I said, "Thanks," but I thought, I outrank you, you southern jerk.

I picked up my seabag and watched the three marines clomp down the stairs. When they got to the landing on the next floor, one of the N.Y./N.J. accents yelled up, "Hey, sailor! Ya wanta get laid?"

I went to the top of the stairs and peered down into the dark. "I beg your pardon?" I said, and the voice answered, "We're going over to Shepherd's Market on a pussy hunt. It's opposite the Christian Science Church on Curzon Street. Come on over if ya get horny."

"Right," I said, "Shepherd's Market opposite the Christian Science Church." I held my thumb up to make him think that we were all in it together, that if I felt the need for some pussy, I would go right to the Christian Science Church, then take a bearing, cross Curzon Street to Shepherd's Market, and join my new roommates. "Right," I said again. This time I winked and joined my thumb and forefinger and made the O sign that I thought was the international signal for "OK." It was pitch-dark and the marines had already started down the stairs. I thought I heard the corporal say, "Swabbie bastard. Whudju invite him for?" but I wasn't sure.

The tweeny's room was small. It would have been small for a tweeny, but for three marines and a first-class navy petty officer, it was totally inadequate. There were two single beds and one three-quarter bed taking up most of the floor space. Over in the corner, under a slanting ceiling, was an army cot covered with knapsacks, toilet articles, marine uniforms, a Japanese flag, and a bottle almost full of Kentucky Tavern bourbon whiskey.

I dropped my seabag and sat on the cot. The air-raid sirens were still wailing and had now been joined by the distant popping sounds of anti-aircraft guns and the deep drone of high-flying aircraft. I thought about home in Santa Monica and my mother and a girl named Dixie Langdon, a dancer in the chorus of *Pal Joey*, then I thought about the three marines and their offer to join them in Shepherd's Market. The more I thought about it, the more churlish it seemed to let them spend their first night in London alone. The German bombers were now dropping their bombs somewhere a long way off, and as I sat there in the dark listening to the soft, mushroom-sounding impacts, I decided that I owed it to the three marine combat veterans to join them. They hadn't let us down in Guadalcanal, and I didn't think I should let them down in Shepherd's Market.

I shaved in the bathroom on the first floor, but I didn't take a bath because they only had cold water and to hell with that. I borrowed some of the marines' Aqua Velva Skin Bracer and sprinkled it under my arms and in my shoes. Then I poured some Vitalis on my hair, wiped my shoes on the backs of my calves, put my hat on, and smiled at myself in the mirror. I dashed down the stairs the way Ronald Colman did in *The Prisoner of Zenda*.

I opened the front door and became seasick immediately. A blanket of pregnant, yellowish fog had descended on Green Street and, as far as I knew, the rest of London. Visibility had been reduced to about ten inches, and the fog was so thick and so oppressive I could almost smell it. There are five steps in the front of No. 87, and when I had walked down three of them, I looked around and couldn't see the house. I held on to the handrail and made it to the sidewalk.

A figure loomed toward me and I said, "Pardon me, sir, but could you show me the way to Curzon Street?"

The figure stopped a few feet away and an American voice said, "Sure, Mac. Ya turn right on Audley Street and keep going till ya get to the end. That's Curzon Street. What address are ya lookin' for?"

I recognized Chief Grotsky's voice, but I didn't think he recognized mine and I knew he couldn't see me. I dropped my voice a couple of octaves and said, "The Christian Science

Church, that's what I'm looking for, the Christian Science Church."

"It's on the left about four blocks down," he said. "Ya can't miss it. The only thing is, it's probably closed this time of night, unless ya just want the reading room. I think that's open all the time."

"That's what I want," I said. "The reading room. If I can just find the Christian Science Reading Room, I'll be OK."

"Well, that's where it is," he said. "Right down at the end of Curzon Street, across from Shepherd's Market."

"Thank you, sir," I said, and hurried off. There was no traffic and no sound, except for the air-raid sirens and the ack-ack guns and the German bombs, and they were all so far away that they didn't seem real. I got to the corner of Audley Street and heard muffled voices coming from the basement at No. 62, the navy mess. I thought about going in, but the mission I was on seemed more important, so I turned right and pressed on.

At the end of Curzon Street, on the left side, just as Chief Grotsky had said, was the Third Church of Christ Scientist. I walked up the steps and stopped on a landing between six giant stone columns. I looked up, and above the door there was a mural that said CLEANSE THE LEPER — RAISE THE DEAD — HEAL THE SICK. Engraved at the base of one of the stone columns was the following: THIRD CHURCH OF CHRIST SCIEN-TIST — LONDON. THIS CORNER-STONE WAS LAID ON 9TH JULY 1910. This reminded me of my mission, so I turned around and looked for Shepherd's Market.

The sirens were still wailing away, the bombs were drop-ping, and the ack-ack guns were firing in the distance, but it never occurred to me that they had anything to do with me. I crossed the street and expected to be confronted by three marines and four French beauties, one for each of them and one for me. Instead, I literally bumped into a policeman stand-ing on the corner of Half Moon and Curzon streets. He was the first London bobby I had seen.

"Pardon me, sir," I said. "Can you tell me how to get to Shepherd's Market?"

He looked at me for a moment and then said, "You're a Yank, ain'tcha?"

"Yes, sir," I said. For some reason, I always said "Yes, sir" to anyone taller than I was or anyone in uniform: train porters, ushers, lion tamers, and so on. "How could you tell?"

"Because you called it Shepherd's Market, with an *s*. There's no *s*. It's named after Mr. Edward Shepherd, who owned most of Mayfair in the eighteenth century."

"Well," I said, "I'd certainly like to take a look at his market."

"There's an air raid on," he said. "You're supposed to take cover."

"Yes, sir," I said. "I thought I might find some cover in Mr. Shepherd's Market."

"Yes, you might do," he said, "but I think you'd be safer in the Green Park tube station or the Red Cross club."

I had been in Red Cross clubs, and they weren't my idea of a place to spend my first night in London. "How do I get to the tube station?" I said.

"Well," he said, "you could go along Half Moon Street here to Piccadilly, turn left to Stratton Street, and there you are. You can't miss it." There seemed to be some kind of rule for when the British are trying to help you find someplace: they are supposed to end each bit of direction with "you can't miss it," especially if it's a place that you could very easily miss.

I said, "Thank you, sir. How far is it?" stalling, hoping he would go away so I could find Mr. Shepherd's Market.

"Not far, really," he said.

Several pedestrians scurried by, headed somewhere — probably Green Park tube station. Finally he said, "You can also get there if you go through Shepherd Market to Whitehorse Street, over to Piccadilly, and left to Stratton Street." He didn't say "you can't miss it" this time.

"That sounds like a better way," I said.

"It's a bit longer," he said, "but you may find it more colorful."

"This is my first night in London," I said, "so the more color the better. Which way is it?"

"Right," he said. I looked right and saw the vague outline of the Christian Science Church looming in the fog. I hadn't yet learned that the British often say "right" instead of clearing their throats just to start a conversation. "Left," he said, and pointed up Curzon Street. "First left, just past the green-grocer's."

I gave him a kind of informal half-salute, which might have

been wrongly interpreted as a cap-tug. He smiled and said, "You can't miss it," and I knew I was back on good terms with him. I thanked him and walked twenty-two steps to an archway with a sign over it, which I could barely read through the fog. It said SHEPHERD MARKET W1, LEADING TO WHITEHORSE STREET AND PICCADILLY — CITY OF WESTMINSTER. I went through the arch and looked at the first door on the left. There were two small, well-polished, brass plates over two doorbells. The top one read STEERING WHEEL CLUB (MEMBERS ONLY — PLEASE RING IF CLOSED). The second read ORDER OF THE ROAD (PLEASE RING IF CLOSED).

There was a third bell and over it was a little card on which had been printed GRETA in green ink. While I was deciding whether or not to ring Greta's bell, someone tapped me on the shoulder. I turned around and saw several ghostlike figures hurrying by, but none of them paid any attention to me. I left the door and walked past the Bunch of Grapes pub and into the main part of Shepherd Market. It was (and is) a charming village quarter of narrow streets and alleys, surrounded by three- and four-story terraced buildings. They may have been brand-new, but with the fog and the mystery and the anticipation, they seemed Dickensian and full of hidden promises. Again I felt a tap on my shoulder. This time I turned around quickly and surprised a small middle-aged woman carrying a shopping bag. She wore a grey scarf over her head.

"I beg your pardon," she said, "but do you mind if I touch your dickey?"

"Are you French?" I said.

"No," she said. "I live in Fulham. It's good luck to touch a sailor's dickey."

"Really?" I said.

"Yes, if you don't mind," she said.

I looked around to see if anyone was watching. We seemed reasonably obscured by the fog so I said, "No, it's OK. Go ahead, ma'm."

She walked around in back of me and tapped my collar, muttered, "God bless you, sailor," and disappeared. I learned later that a sailor's collar is called a dickey, and that since Lord Nelson's time it has been considered good luck to tap it and say "God bless you, sailor."

This wasn't exactly what I had anticipated in Shepherd

Market, and I was standing there debating whether to go back to the tweeny's room in Green Street or to the Green Park tube station or the Red Cross club, when a voice with a French accent said, "Bon soir, handsome." I turned around and there was a genuine French whore. I could tell because she had a patent-leather handbag and wore high heels and lots of makeup. She was quite old, and despite the soft, fog-filtered, flattering half-light, she was shockingly ugly. Even if she had had all of her front teeth she would have been no beauty.

"You are looking for a beautiful girl to make love to?" she said.

"Well, no, ma'm, not really," I said. "I was actually looking for three buddies of mine, marines. Two tall ones and one short one. They told me to meet 'em in Shepherd Market. You haven't seen 'em, have you?"

"Are you sure you don't want to make love, darling?" she said coyly.

I looked around and saw the bobby's silhouette standing in the archway. "Not tonight," I said. "Not in all this fog. I just got into town and I want to find my buddies. Maybe another time, after the fog lifts."

"I think you are shy," she said. "I think you are a Yankee and I think you are shy."

"No," I said. "I'm not shy. Tell me where I can find you and I'll come around another time and prove I'm not shy."

"I bet you won't come," she said.

"I'll bet I will," I said.

"How much?" she said.

"A pound," I said. "I'll bet you a pound."

"Make it two pounds, sailor, and come to see Greta. Greta over the greengrocer's."

The bobby started to walk toward us and Greta melted away in the fog.

"Are you having trouble finding Whitehorse Street?" he said as he reached my side.

"It's around here someplace," I said. "It's just the fog. Can't see a thing." He stood there, so I thought I'd better say something more, in the interests of Anglo-American relations. "This is my first air raid," I said. "First time I've heard the air-raid sirens and the first time I've heard bombs falling." The bobby didn't say anything, so I said, "This is also my first experience with your famous London fog."

"Why don't you try the Red Cross club?" he said. "It's closer than the tube station."

"Where is it?" I said.

"Across the street, next to the church," he said. "It's called the Washington Club. It's for American enlisted men. No officers allowed. Only enlisted men and pretty Red Cross girls. They serve hot dogs and doughnuts and coffee and hot chocolate, and they have dancing."

"Well, thanks, officer," I said. "Maybe I'll give it a look later."

"If I were you, I'd look in now," he said. "They close early. Come along, I'll take you over."

Today, at 7 Curzon Street, London W1, there is a lively, reasonably priced hotel called the Washington. As you enter, on the right, a sign on the door to the bar says THE FOURTH HUSSAR. On the left is the reception and a lift, a bit farther along on the right is a comfortable lobby full of the kind of people who fill up lobbies in reasonably priced West End hotels. There is no music in the lobby, not even discreet Muzak.

In 1942, No. 7 was still the Washington, but it was called the Washington Club instead of the Washington Hotel, the lobby was filled with American soldiers, sailors, and marines, Red Cross girls, and volunteer English lady hostesses ("Help a Yank to help you"), and the walls reverberated with the triple nasal sounds of the Andrews Sisters belting out "Don't Sit Under the Apple Tree with Anyone Else but Me." A few GI's danced and played Ping-Pong with a few Red Cross girls, but most of them lounged on the furniture reading *Yank*, *Stars and Stripes*, or some dog-eared comic books, which, according to the sign on the reading table, had been provided by the "Make the Yanks Feel at Home Committee." There was also a set of Dickens, some old copies of *Punch*, a stack of Christian Science literature, and some ancient *National Geographic* magazines.

As I came in, the Andrews Sisters had reached full stride and a group of GI's with pimples were standing around the record player, singing along and snapping their fingers. A fat

Red Cross girl sang with them, her eyes closed in ecstasy, and the flat-heeled, no-nonsense shoe on her right foot tapped in rhythm with her shaking head. She was in heaven, which was better than being in Waverly, Ohio, or wherever she came from.

The main action was at a snack bar—cafeteria at the far end of the lobby. I went over to the food counter and a beautiful, mature English volunteer worker served me. She was about thirty years old and had a lovely upper-class voice. When I asked for a ham sandwich and a cup of hot chocolate, she said, "Would you like a digestive biscuit with your hot chocolate?" I had never had a digestive biscuit, and it sounded like a cure for a hangover or an upset stomach. I didn't have either, but the volunteer worker was so pretty that I said, "Yes, that would be fine." She gave me a round, flat, brownish cracker. I said, "Thank you, ma'm," and she said, "There's a table in the corner." I looked around and saw a table for two tucked away in the shadows between the Ping-Pong table and the "Have you written home to-day?" desk, and I said, "Would you like to join me?" She said, "I'll come over in a minute," which she did.

Her name turned out to be Lady Caroline, and she told me it was part of her job to make all of the American visitors feel at home. I told her that I didn't know about the rest of the Americans, but that I felt at home already, mainly because she was so friendly, but also because my first love, a part-Indian girl from Colorado, had been named Caroline. Lady Caroline asked me to tell her about the Indian Caroline, and I did and she seemed really interested.

After I finished my hot chocolate, Lady Caroline went back to work at the food counter while I played Ping-Pong with the fat Red Cross girl, who turned out to be from Hailey, Idaho, instead of Waverly, Ohio. She said her name was Hilda and that she could ski and hunt and fish, and I believed her. If she had told me that she was an Olympic champion weight lifter and free-fall wrestler, I'd have believed that too. She had beaten me four games and worked up quite a sweat, when she threw the paddle on the table and said we'd play some more when she got back from "freshening up" in the ladies' room. I was looking around for a way to be not available, when I noticed Lady Caroline coming out from behind the food counter with her coat on. I asked her if she was leaving and she said, "Yes, would you like to walk me home?" I said I would like that very much, which was the truth and had nothing to do with my not wanting to be there when Hilda came back from the ladies' room, freshened up, but still fat.

Lady Caroline lived in a charming house in Hays Mews. She had a butler, a coal fire, and a bottle of brandy. She probably had a lot of other things, but these are the things I noticed. The butler was obviously expecting her, because the fire was glowing and the brandy bottle and one glass were set out on the table in front of the fire. The butler's name was Albert, and after she said, "Good evening, Albert," and he said, "Good evening, madam," he took our coats, put another brandy glass on the table, and disappeared.

Lady Caroline said, "Do you like brandy?"

I had never tasted brandy so I said, "Brandy's fine with me."

"I'm afraid this is the last bottle," she said. As she sat down in front of the fire, I had a chance to look at her legs for the first time. They were long and perfectly shaped, and I fell in love with her. Not just her long, perfectly shaped legs. Her. All of her, from the trim ankles to the coal fire and the brandy and the wood paneling in the room and the butler and the digestive biscuits at the Washington Club and her softness and her eyes and her hair and, Christ, I hoped there was nobody in the house except her and me and the goddamn butler.

"How long have you been in the navy?" she said.

"Eleven months," I said. "I went on active service the day after Pearl Harbor."

"My husband's been in the navy since he was sixteen," she said. "His uncle is Admiral of the Fleet."

Bully for him and his uncle, I thought, but I said, "Gee, Admiral of the Fleet. Which fleet?"

"Well, at the beginning of the war he was in the Med, but now he's in the Pacific, and Jeremy's in the North Atlantic on a destroyer."

"Is Jeremy your husband?" I said.

"Yes," she said, and she burst into tears and put her hands to her eyes.

I gulped my brandy and poked the coal fire and looked at

the oil painting on the wall. It was a still life with some dead rabbits and two ducks, also dead. Then it stopped being a still life because in the corner there was a guy in a red coat blowing a trumpet.

"When did you last hear from your husband?" I asked. "Is he still in the North Atlantic?"

"I guess so," she said. "I haven't heard from him for some time."

I stared into the fire for a while and then I said, "Do you live alone here?"

"Well, yes, I do now," she said. "Except when Jeremy's in London. Aside from him, there's only Albert, he's the butler, and the housekeeper and the two maids."

"I suppose they're all asleep now," I said.

"Yes, I suppose they are," she said. "Would you like another brandy?"

I looked at the bottle and saw that there was about one inch left so I said, "No thanks. One stiff brandy is about all I can take, especially on top of hot chocolate and digestive biscuits. I'd better be getting back to Eighty-seven Green Street before they lock me out."

Lady Caroline came with me to the door and said, "Thanks for seeing me home."

"It was my pleasure," I said.

"Will you come to the club tomorrow night?" she said.

"Yes," I said. "What time?"

"Whatever time you get there, I'll be there," she said.

I took her in my arms and she began to sob uncontrollably. I kissed her neck, under her left ear because that's where my mouth was. "I'll be there too," I said.

She didn't say anything, but I could feel her warm tears on my throat, under my black silk sailor's tie. I held her for a few moments, and then I kissed her forehead, opened the door, and found myself enveloped in the fog in Hays Mews.

On the walk back from Hays Mews a gentle wind began to blow, and by the time I reached Grosvenor Square the fog had almost completely disappeared. The air-raid sirens were still moaning and a few falling bombs could still be heard, but they no longer sounded like popping mushrooms. They sounded more like someone coughing in the far distance. There was a fence around Grosvenor Square, and behind the fence were British soldiers and anti-aircraft guns. Some long cables from barrage balloons were anchored there, on the north side, where the statue of Franklin D. Roosevelt is now. These small captive balloons were used to support cables or nets as a protection against air attacks. The stock American serviceman's joke was that the balloons were holding the island up, and that if you cut the cables, it would sink because of the heavy armaments being brought in by the Americans. After sampling British cooking, some of the GI's looked favorably on this cable-cutting idea, and it was rumored that pliers were issued at the PX in case an opportunity to prove the theory came up. I'm not sure that the British were particularly worried about this, but I am sure that I was not allowed to walk through Grosvenor Square where the balloons were anchored.

Now that the fog was gone, I could also see gaping holes where buildings had been bombed during the Battle of Britain over two years before. A house on the west side of Grosvenor Square, where the new American embassy is now, had been completely demolished except for the staircase, which now reached up five or six stories into the black night. The side of another house had been blasted away, leaving a neat cross-section view of each of the rooms on five floors. The only thing out of place was the toilet bowl on the landing between the first floor and the second floor. It was hanging out into space, suspended by two small copper pipes that were still attached to the plumbing.

When I arrived at the fifth floor landing at 87 Green Street, I heard some movement inside the tweeny's room. I knocked, and a girl's voice said, "Come in." I opened the door and saw a very pretty young girl brushing a U.S. Marine uniform that was hanging from a wire that had been strung up over the single window. My extra suit of dress blues hung beside it, and two other marine uniforms hung on a second wire that had been strung up over the bottom half of the window. Most of the spoor that the three marines and I had left scattered around was neatly folded on the foot of the beds, and three bayonets and four helmets hung on hooks on the wall. Three glasses and a blue-and-white porcelain pitcher of water had been placed on the table in the center of the room, and next to them was a matching porcelain candle holder with a burning candle. The bottle of Kentucky Tavern bourbon was in front of the candle, and the soft, flickering backlight made it seem bigger than it was.

"It's not a proper blackout curtain," said the girl, "but it'll do in a pinch, won't it?"

"Yes," I said. "I guess it will." Then I said, "Any old port in a storm."

"I guess you're the sailor in the group," she said.

"Yes, I am," I said. "That's my uniform hanging over the top half of the window."

"You're the first sailor I've had up here," she said.

I thought, Well, you haven't had me yet, and I began to wonder how I could correct this situation. She gave the marine uniform a final swipe with the brush and leaned over to sort out some marine olive-green dirty underwear. The T-shirts and shorts had obviously been worn a long time without being laundered, and they were sweaty and probably stank. If they did, the girl didn't seem to notice it. Her full bosom kind of popped out over her blouse like it did in Elizabethan paintings, and I tried to look down the crease between her breasts. All I could see was the top of her head. Her soft, dark hair was parted in the middle and combed neatly back like a madonna's. I moved closer to see if I could get a better angle on her breasts, but before I could see anything she stood up and said, "Do you have any laundry you would like to have done?" I knew I had two pairs of dirty shorts and a dirty T-shirt around somewhere, but I didn't want this young, pretty girl to become involved with them so I said, "No, I'm all laundered up-to-date, clean as a whistle. Who are you?"

"I'm the maid," she said. "My aunt and uncle were the butler and housekeeper here before the war and I was the up-stairs maid. This used to be my room. They moved to the country and I stayed to work for the Americans. My name is Molly." She started toward the door.

"Would you like a drink?" I said. She stopped and I said, "Would you like a drink of Kentucky Tavern bourbon?"

"I've never tasted bourbon," she said. "I'm not sure I'd like it."

"How're you going to know unless you try?" I said.

"I'd better not," she said. "I have to do this laundry, and then at midnight I have to make coffee for the officers. They change the watch at the Navy Headquarters at midnight, and then they want coffee and then they sit around and talk. I like to listen to them."

"It's only nine o'clock," I said. "Why don't you talk to me, and then later you can go down and listen to the officers."

"What about the laundry?" she said.

"That's marine laundry," I said. "They don't like it washed. They usually powder it."

"What do you mean?" she said.

I took the marine helmet with two chevrons painted on it from the hook on the wall and said, "Put it in here and I'll show you."

She dropped the dirty underwear into the helmet. "Now fill two glasses half-full of bourbon," I said, "and I'll get the powder."

She said, "Are you sure?" but this was only after she had opened the bottle and poured the first drink.

"Positive," I said. I got a can of delousing powder out of my seabag and sprinkled it generously into the marine helmet. Then I took one of the marines' bayonets off the wall and stirred the dirty underwear around as though it were a stew.

"When do I pour the bourbon in?" said Molly.

"You don't pour it in," I said. "You put some water in with the bourbon, and after I finish powdering the marine underwear we'll have our little drink." I kept stirring until the fabric had absorbed the powder, then I dumped the underwear on the floor, kicked it under one of the beds, and hung the helmet and bayonet back on the wall. "That's why they make marine underwear green," I said, "so the marines won't know when it's dirty."

"Do all marines powder their underwear?" she said.

"No," I said, "only the clean ones, the guys who stand guard duty at the embassy. The real combat marines wear 'em until they snap and crackle, then they shake 'em down into the combat boots."

"How much water should I pour in?" she asked.

"Just a touch in mine," I said, "but I don't think you should put any in yours. Not if you've never tasted bourbon." She poured a splash of water from the porcelain pitcher into one of the glasses and handed it to me, then she picked up her half-glass of straight 100-proof bourbon, touched my glass with it, and said, "Cheers."

I held my glass up the way Rex Harrison did in *Blithe Spirit* and said, "Down the hatch."

"Welcome to Britain," she said, and swallowed the bourbon with one gulp.

I watched her beautiful brown English eyes fill with tears, then glaze over and fill up again. "Would you like a sip of water?" I said. She didn't answer, but she sat down on my cot, which I thought was a step in the right direction. I poured some water into the third glass, sat down beside her, and held it to her lips. She sipped it gratefully and said perhaps she had drunk the bourbon too fast. I agreed and said that maybe it would be better to have some water with the next one. She looked at me and smiled and I smiled back and said, "Here, try mine, it's not as strong."

"No more," she said.

"Why not?" I said.

She leaned over and kissed me under the ear where I had kissed Lady Caroline and said, "Because I don't like to make love when I'm drunk."

I was about to say, "Neither do I," and take her in my arms, but I had a glass in each hand. I got up to put them on the table and she got up too. She crossed to the door, opened it, and said, "I'll be back."

"Why?" I said. "You're already here. Why go away and come back if you're already here in the first place?"

"I have to get something," she said. Then she put her arms around me and kissed me full on the lips. I started to open my mouth to tell her that I still had the glasses in my hands and that if she would give me a moment I would put them on the table and kiss her properly. As soon as my lips parted, she slid her soft, warm tongue into my mouth, and I dropped the glasses and put both arms around her. We kissed in the doorway for quite a while, rubbing up against each other and crunching our feet around on the broken glass. She kept saying she had to go get something, and I kept trying to get her back into the room and onto the cot. She said she would not come back into the room until she got what she said she had to get, and I finally decided it was some kind of contraceptive and began to think maybe it wasn't such a bad idea. If she had been around 87 Green Street for long, who knows what she might have picked up, especially from the officers on the first floor, to say nothing of the CPO's in the basement?

"OK," I said, "I'll stand right here until you come back." She gave me a final, passionate kiss, and I rubbed my hands over her breasts, and she put her tongue in my ear, and I rubbed my hand down her belly, and she said, "Please don't," and put her hand on my hand and guided it even farther down until I felt a soft-hard mound through her dress. She put her tongue into my ear again, and while it was there she said "Please, don't" again, and the middle of her body, down where she was pressing my hand, began to move, but the top part of her body remained quiet except for her "Please don'ts" and her heavy breathing. She started to rub my belly with her other hand and I said, "Ohmygod," and her breath came faster and I closed my eyes and said "Ohmygod" again and then she disappeared.

At first I thought she was just standing back, resting for another attack. I kept my eyes closed and groped out for her, and then I heard her footsteps running down the stairs. I stood there feeling like a jerk for the second time that night — or, if I included Lady Caroline *and* Greta over the greengrocer, for the third time.

I wasn't sure if Molly would be back with or without a contraceptive or whatever in the hell she was so anxious to get, but I thought if she did come back nude or in a nightgown, she would probably be barefooted. I didn't want her to have to walk through the broken glass, so I got the pile of marine underwear and swept the glass under the bed with it, then I stripped down to my underwear and got under the covers on the cot and waited.

I didn't only wait, of course: I also stared at the ceiling and sweated and reassured myself that she would soon be back with her goddamn rubbers or fishskins or whatever they used in England. I listened in vain for the slightest sound and finally convinced myself that she had teased me and run out on me. I got up and took another slug of bourbon from the bottle. I thought I heard someone laughing somewhere in the house, so I dived back under the covers. I worried about Molly having to make coffee for the officers at midnight when it was already 9:30. Then I thought that the three marines might come in, and that wouldn't be my idea of a jolly evening. When I thought about the marines, I thought about their underwear full of ground glass and delousing powder and I laughed to myself. Then I stopped laughing because it suddenly occurred to me that the underwear I was wearing was probably dirty. I knew I had a clean pair in my seabag, so I jumped out of the cot, took the dirty pair off, and was bending over, with my head in the seabag, when I heard the door close behind me. I turned around and saw Molly standing inside the door, fully dressed.

She laughed and said, "You're tanned. The American navy must go in for sunbathing." I quickly held the seabag up in front of me and she laughed again and said, "Here's what I had to get." She showed me a key, which she then turned to lock the door. "When this was my room," she said, "I locked the door every night, as soon as I came in."

"I don't blame you," I said. "You can't be too careful."

"Get into bed," she said.

"I was just looking for something," I said.

"Whatever it is, you won't need it," she said.

I said she was probably right and dropped the seabag. She smiled and said, "I know I'm right. You've got everything you need. Now are you going to get into bed, or are you going to stand there shivering?"

I got back under the covers and Molly poured some bourbon into the last unbroken glass and then filled it with water. She knelt beside the bed and held the glass to my lips. She watched me take a deep drink, with the glass chattering against my front teeth, and then she gave me a tender kiss on my wet lips. Then I watched her take a deep drink, and I gave her a tender kiss on her wet lips. She put the glass beside my cot and undressed slowly and deliberately and provocatively, stopping now and then to take another sip of bourbon and to kiss me. She finally removed her last bit of clothing and stood in front of the candle. She was even more beautiful than I had imagined. She was stunning. Or in any event, I was stunned, and I think any frustrated, red-blooded twenty-two-year-old sailor in the U.S. Navy who had experienced what I had experienced that night would have been just as stunned. I watched, trying to keep my bottom jaw from slacking open as she came over to my cot, picked up the glass, refilled it, and calmly crossed over and sat on the widest of the three other beds.

"It's more comfortable over here," she said. She took some pins out of her hair and it fell down over her shoulders. She turned the covers down and lay back on the bed. I was in no mood to argue the point, so I went over and lay down beside her and pulled the covers over us. I took her in my arms and we picked up where we had left off when she had gone to get the key, only now we were lying in a warm, comfortable bed with the door locked instead of standing in a cold hall in broken glass. We made love as though we had both done it before, which we both had, but never like that. Afterward, I held her in my arms and she went to sleep for a while, and then we made love again and drank some more of the marines' bourbon. Molly lit a cigarette and I said, "What's a tweeny?"

"A tweeny is a maid who works between floors," she said. She put her cigarette out and took a sip of bourbon. "Tweeny. Between. Get it?"

"Got it," I said.

She kissed me and said, "I love my first American sailor."

"I love my first ex-tweeny," I said. "You are the first ex-tweeny I've ever made love to by candlelight, during an air raid."

"We're lucky," she said. "Good lovemaking is mostly luck." She got up and started to dress. "Everything in life is mostly luck, timing, happening to be in the right place at the right time, happening to find a bottle of bourbon and a charming sailor who happens to be the best lovemaker in the United States Navy."

She was standing with her back to me, buttoning her blouse. "Would you like to touch my dickey?" I said. "That's supposed to be lucky." She turned and looked at me and smiled. "It's hanging over the window," I said.

"It's only lucky when a sailor's wearing it," she said. "Besides, I've been lucky enough for one evening. I don't want to be greedy." She picked up the empty bourbon bottle and said, "No need to leave this here."

I watched her and thought, Oh, Christ, she's going to go away. She's going to go downstairs and make coffee for a lot of snotty officers, and then she's going to listen to their bullshit and forget about me.

She unlocked the door and stood there for a moment, looking at me. "It's almost twelve o'clock," she said. "Your friends should be here soon. There's a curfew, you know." I got out of bed and took her in my arms, and we kissed passionately for the last time. "Get some sleep," she whispered, and she was gone.

I straightened the marine's bed and crawled into the cold cot under the slanting ceiling. I was reliving the evening when the door opened and Molly slipped in and sat on the side of the cot. She held up a full bottle of Southern Comfort. "I found this in the officers' quarters," she said. "Is it the same as bourbon?"

"Close enough," I said.

She kissed me tenderly and said, "Sleep well. Thanks for everything."

"Forget it," I said. "It's nothing. Only the best night of my life, so far."

She put the bottle of Southern Comfort on the table, kissed me again, blew out the candle, and left the room.

The ack-ack and the bombs were now so far away that I could hardly hear them.

"Gimme the fuckin' flashlight."

"Grotsky said we ain't allowed to have lights in the room. There ain't no blackout curtains."

"Fuck 'im. He's fulla shit. He said we was sure to get laid in Shepherd's Market and instead we fuckin' near got thrown in the brig."

"That was because you kicked in the door of the fruit and vegetable store."

"Greengrocer's. That's what they call 'em over here."

"That's not what she said. She said her *name* was Greta Greengrocer."

"Bullshit, she said Greta *over* the greengrocer. If you hadn't started kicking in the greengrocer's door, we'da all got laid."

"Fuckin' bobby."

"He let us off, didn't he?"

"Fuck 'im."

"Gimme a cigarette."

I heard a match strike, and I kept my face to the wall and snorted and breathed heavily.

"Where'd the candle come from?"

"Beats the shit outa me."

"Lookit this. Our uniforms are hung up over the window."

"Light the candle."

"How about that. The fuckin' swabbie cleaned up the room and made the beds."

"He must be a fag."

"I told ya. I knew it when he wanted to share a bed. Fuckin' pervert."

"No wonder he didn't want to come out with us and get laid."

"Only we didn't get laid."

"Well, he don't know that and we ain't gonna tell him. Fag bastard. Where's my bottle of Kentucky Tavern?"

"On the table."

"I'm sackin' out."

"Me too."

"Don'tcha want a drink?"

"Not that shit."

I heard the bottle being opened and pretended to snore a little bit. A few seconds later there was a violent hacking and coughing, and a mouthful of Southern Comfort was sprayed around the room.

"Cocksucker!"

"What's ya problem, Lamar?"

"This ain't my bourbon."

"Whose bourbon is it?"

"Will you guys knock it off, for Christ's sakes?"

"It's Southern Comfort."

"That's a fag drink. Must be the swabbie's."

"Where's my Kentucky Tavern?"

One of the N.Y./N.J. marines started to snore and the other one said, "Goodnight, Lamar."

There was a long silence, and then I heard Lamar gulp down a drink of Southern Comfort. I turned over fitfully and continued my heavy breathing and snoring. I threw my right arm over my face and peeked out and saw Lamar sitting there in the candlelight. He took another long pull at the bottle, stripped down to his green shorts and tattoos, and crawled into the bed where Molly and I had made love. After a few minutes one of the N.Y./N.J. marines said, "You forgot to blow out the candle."

"How would you like to blow it out your ass, Al?" said Lamar.

"You were the last one up," said Al.

"Blow it out your ass," said Lamar.

"You already said that," said Al.

They argued about who was going to blow the candle out until Lamar had said "Blow it out your ass" about ten more times and Al had started to snore. Lamar lay there for a while, and then he got up, took another belt of Southern Comfort, blew out the candle, and stood there in the middle of the room. The room was pitch-dark and silent except for the distant sounds of the air raid, my rhythmic breathing, and the snoring of the N.Y./N.J. marines. I opened my eyes wide but couldn't see a thing. There wasn't a sliver of moonlight coming through Molly's blackout curtain.

Lamar let out an explosive fart and Al woke up and said, "Did you get any on you?" Lamar farted again and giggled, and I heard him take two steps toward his bed and then let out an ungodly scream. The third marine sat up and shined his flashlight on Lamar. "What the fuck is going on?" he said.

Lamar was holding his left foot and hopping around on his right. He was yelling "fuckass" and "shitass" and "cocksucker" and things like that, and when the beam of light settled on his left foot, I could see blood oozing from between his toes. "Some asshole sprinkled glass around, and I've cut my fuckin' foot off," he said. "That's what's going on."

"Give the man a Purple Heart," said one of the N.Y./N.J. voices.

The ack-ack guns and the bombing finally stopped altogether, and after a few moments I heard the long, low whine of the all-clear siren.

I closed my eyes and thought of England.

71–72 Grosvenor Street, London W1

The building at 71–72 Grosvenor Street, London W1, is seven stories high and made of solid brick. There are two entrances, both with heavy mahogany doors. In the middle of each door there is a polished brass lion's head with a brass ring in its mouth, and above each door there is an iron grille with a number in the center.

In 1942 the No. 71 door was closed and a sign read PLEASE ENTER NO. 72. Inside No. 72, a crippled security guard asked to see my identification card. In those days 71–72 Grosvenor Street was the London headquarters of the OSS. Two blocks from Grosvenor Square, it was close enough, but not too close, to the United States embassy, which was at 1 Grosvenor Square (where the Canadian embassy is now), and to the U.S. Navy headquarters, which was (and still is) at 18 Grosvenor Square.

After being checked by the security guard, I presented my orders to the OSS duty officer, an army captain whose name I have forgotten. He wrote my name and time of arrival in the logbook and said, "Field Photographic is on the second floor, that's third floor American. The ground floor doesn't have a number over here."

I started to ask why, but he looked like the kind of guy who wouldn't know but would tell me anyway, so I thanked him and took the elevator to the second floor. There were no signs on any of the doors, but I heard some laughing coming from behind one of them. I knocked, the laughing stopped, and an American voice said, "Come in."

I opened the door and found six friends of mine from the OSS in Washington. They had been in England several months and were full of questions about what was going on at home and information about what was going on here. They kidded me about not coming over until they had made it safe for me, then they asked me about my "stopover" in Ireland. I was about to give them some colorful details, when Comdr. Ford walked in. He was wearing a pair of unpressed grey pants, brown-and-white saddle shoes, a rumpled grey coat with the collar turned up all around, and a grey felt hat with the brim turned down all around. He had a pipe in his mouth and he wore dimly smoked glasses. He was in the OSS and we were allowed to wear civilian clothes, but he had gone too far. He looked like a badly wardrobed character out of Sean O'Casey.

I was wearing my dress blues with a blue turtleneck sweater under the middy blouse. This was not strictly regulation, but it was acceptable if the weather was cold enough. I soon found out that English weather is very changeable and that some-time during any day it's usually cold enough or hot enough for any kind of clothing. Ford muttered a general good morning without looking at any of us and walked through a door at the other end of the room. The door closed behind him, then it opened again and he came out, crossed over to where I was standing, and pulled at my turtleneck sweater.

"You're out of uniform," he said. "As soon as you have the uniform of the day, I'd like to see you in my office." I said, "Yessir," and he turned and went back through the door. When he was gone we all rolled our eyes and shook our fingers and made silent gestures that indicated that the old man was in a bad mood and that we all faced a rough day. I took off my turtleneck sweater and knocked on Ford's door. "Come in," he said. I opened the door. Ford was sitting in a swivel chair with his stockinged feet on the desk.

"How was your trip?" he said.

"Very interesting, sir."

"No trouble?"

"No, sir."

He looked at me through the smoked glasses, filled his pipe, and said, "How did you like Ireland?"

"Fine," I said. "It's a fine country. I liked it very much."

He lit his pipe and said, "I thought you would." The pipe went out and he relit it. "Did you bring the film?" he said.

"Yessir."

"Good lad," he said. "We'll run it at the admiralty tonight at nineteen hundred hours. I want you to come with me and Lt. Kellogg." Kellogg was his executive officer.

I said, "Yessir," but I was thinking about my date with Lady Caroline at the Washington Club.

He leaned over, took one of his socks off, and started to scratch the bottom of his foot. "Did you have any trouble with the Irish customs?" he said.

"No, sir," I said. "No trouble at all."

He stopped scratching and looked directly into my eyes and smiled. "OK, Parrish," he finally said. "Dismissed." I saluted and started to leave. "Parrish," he said. I stopped, turned around, and stood at attention. "Take some time off this afternoon and read the Bluejackets Manual," he said. "Pay particular attention to the chapter on saluting when you're not wearing a hat."

"Yessir," I said. I almost saluted again, but decided not to.

8

Active Duty

I spent the next three years of the war on active duty in England, continental Europe, and Washington. Some duty was more active than other duty. For example, I married a pretty San Francisco Red Cross girl named Kathleen Thompson, made a documentary film at Oxford University in England, and went through a commando-training course in Scotland. Of these three exercises, the commando-training course was the most active, making the documentary was the most educational, and marrying the pretty San Francisco Red Cross girl named Kathleen Thompson was the best thing that ever happened to me in my whole life.

In 1944 and 1945 I flew back and forth across the Atlantic several times for various reasons. I photographed British and American troops in southern England preparing for the invasion of France, and, in March 1945, with a partner, Bob Moreno, I photographed the crossing of the Ludendorff Railway Bridge over the Rhine River at Remagen.

We were assigned to the Ninth Armored Division of the First Army under Gen. Hodges. We arrived at Remagen at 3:00 A.M. on the ninth of March, and all hell was breaking loose. The Germans were trying to blow up the bridge before the Americans could get across. There was heavy fire from both directions across the river. The Germans had been in Remagen for several days before we got there and had dug some foxholes on the grounds of a big resort hotel near the west end of the bridge.

Moreno and I were armed with .45-calibre service pistols and three or four cameras each. We were too far away to fire at the enemy, and it was too dark to take pictures, so we threw the cameras in our weapons carrier and each dived for a foxhole. I say "dived," but what I really mean is that we jumped in, feetfirst. Good thing, too, especially in my foxhole. The bottom was covered with about ten inches of German shit. The previous tenant had apparently lived in it for several days without sticking his head above ground level. I yelled across at Moreno to ask if his foxhole had turned out to be a shithole too, but he didn't answer. The German fire from across the river had suddenly changed from rifle fire to anti-aircraft and machine-gun fire, which swept the area just above our heads and kept us standing in our foxholes with our heads ducked and our knees bent all night.

Just before dawn we crept out and ran into the cellar of the hotel, where a mixed bag of about fifteen German soldiers and civilians was huddled at one end of the room and three GI's with drawn carbines were sitting on wine cases at the other. A pile of German rifles was lying on the floor behind the GI's. It was still dark, and the basement was dramatically lit with candles and army flashlights. One of the GI's, a sergeant, took a slug from a bottle of Rhine wine and looked up at us. Moreno and I were still wearing our green navy parkas and didn't look like soldiers from any army. The sergeant swung his carbine toward me.

"Hi, sarge," I said, and he said, "Who shit?"

I described the foxhole I had spent the night in and said we were U.S. Navy petty officers.

"Well, you get your asses over with the krauts until you get cleaned up," he said.

When daylight came, we turned the German "prisoners of war" over to some MP's and thanked the sergeant for his hospitality. We got our cameras from our weapons carrier and went about our job. We took movies and still pictures of the Americans crossing the bridge. We got an LCVP (Landing Craft, Vehicles and Personnel) and cruised the river, taking pictures of the explosives being removed from the underside of the bridge. We stayed in Remagen until the bridge finally collapsed from the heavy traffic some days later.

We then headed back to Paris, as ordered. We joined Gen. Patton's Third Army at Oberwesel and stayed with them for four days, during which time we saw some combat. Not a lot, but enough.

During my German tour of duty, I saw some dead Germans and some live Germans, but the first ones I recognized were Field Marshal Herman Göring, Adm. Karl Dönitz, Gen. Alfred Jodl, Albert Speer, Rudolf Hess, von Ribbentrop, von Schirach, Keitel, Streicher, and other prominent Nazis. They were taking their daily walk around the exercise yard at Spandau Prison in Nuremberg. I watched them every day from a second-story window overlooking the yard.

After VE Day in May 1945, Comdr. Ford had assigned me and Budd Schulberg, Joe Zigman, and Bob Webb to Justice Jackson's Office for the Prosecution of the Major Nazi War Criminals at Nuremberg. We were given copies of legal briefs indicting Göring and the others and ordered to scour Europe for photographic evidence to confirm the accusations against each man and then to present our film at the trials four months hence.

We found some of the material in the UFA film library and at the Afifa lab in Berlin. UFA was the largest film studio in Germany and the Afifa was the largest film laboratory. Other bits came from Warsaw, Cologne, Zurich, Munich, and wherever else we could winkle them out of the shambles that was Europe in 1945.

In Justice Jackson's "Crimes Against Humanity" brief, great stress was placed on the abortive July 20, 1944, plot on Hitler's life. We knew that the Nazis had photographed every detail of the bloody reprisals, and we knew our allies, the Russians, had the film. What we didn't know was how to get it away from them. We had explained, at every level, that we were all in it together, that our common cause was to punish the villains who had bombed Stalingrad, perpetrated the Holocaust, and generally made life miserable for millions of innocent people for the past ten years. The Russians were polite but firm. They drank and talked with us for hours, but when it was all sifted out, it was still "Nyet." We had lots of conversation, vodka, and bourbon, but no film.

The Russian liaison officer with our group was a Major Gromoff. We wined and dined him and tried to bribe him with everything our overstocked PX offered: cigarettes (more valuable than currency), film, cameras, watches, field glasses, etc. He accepted all the gifts, but I guess we didn't officially bribe him because, when you bribe somebody, they're supposed to deliver something from their side. The major took it all in like a Russian sponge but gave nothing. He spoke perfect English, and when we asked him about the July 20 film, he said he had never heard of it.

Actually, he was a rather nice guy and liked to visit our headquarters in Wannsee, a beautiful suburb of Berlin. It had been in the Russian sector at first, but after Potsdam the areas were changed, and we inherited a fine German mansion that had belonged to Baron von Hanfstangel. The staff included a great cook who spoke some Russian and wasn't bad-looking. Major Gromoff used to hang around, eating our rations and talking to the cook.

One night, Schulberg and I were talking about John Ford, our absent commander. Gromoff heard us and said, "You don't mean John Ford, the great film director?"

"That's right," I said.

He couldn't believe it. "John Ford who made *The Informer* and *Grapes of Wrath?*"

"And *Young Mr. Lincoln*. And *Stagecoach*," Budd said.

"And *The Iron Horse* and *Four Sons* and *Men Without Women* and *The Lost Patrol* and . . ." He went on, naming, in chronological order, every picture that Ford had directed, including some that Schulberg and I hadn't heard of. He was a proper, died-in-the-wool, card-carrying John Ford–film buff. He knew more about Ford, I think, than Ford knew about himself. He flavored his recital with names of the cast and crew of each picture and little-known bits of information: "Ford changed his billing from Jack Ford to John Ford in 1923, when he directed *Cameo Kirby*, starring John Gilbert and Gertrude Olmstead. George Schneiderman was the cameraman, and some of the sequences were tinted, a process used by Ford again in *Mother Machree* in 1928."

"Yes," I said, "but Chester Lyons was the cameraman on *Mother Machree*. I know because I worked in it as a child."

"You've met John Ford?" said the unbelieving Russian.

"Of course. He's our commanding officer, our boss. He's actually in charge of this operation."

"Will he come to Berlin?"

"Probably. We're expecting him any day." That was true, but we had no idea when, or if, he would actually appear.

"He's my hero," said Gromoff. "I'm writing the definitive book about him. In Russian. I'd give anything to meet him."

"Would you give us the July twentieth film?"

"Of course," he said without batting an eye. "You didn't tell me it was for John Ford."

The next day, we took a four-wheel weapons carrier to a warehouse in the Russian zone and Major Gromoff personally supervised the loading of thirty thousand feet of film, everything we needed.

Ford never appeared in Berlin, but I got a photograph of him directing George O'Brien in *The Iron Horse* from the ruins of the bombed-out Twentieth Century–Fox distribution office and forged Ford's signature on it:

> *To Major Gromoff*
> *With gratitude,*
> *John Ford*

We completed our thirteen-hour documentary, titled it *The Nazi Plan,* and turned it in to Justice Jackson's office. During the trials, the prosecution lawyers would present specific arguments against each defendant, then a section of film confirming the arguments would be shown. In some cases, witnesses were called to swear that they were present when the photographs were actually taken.

When my duty was finished at Nuremberg, I returned to Washington, on December 9, 1945, four years and one day after I had been put on active duty in the U.S. Navy. I was discharged at the U.S. Navy Personnel Separation Center at Bainbridge, Maryland.

The next day Kathie and I bought a secondhand black Mercury convertible, named it Witch Boy, and took off for Hollywood and life in the movie business. I got my old job back as an assistant film editor at Universal Studio, and Kathie got a new job as a story editor at the same studio. We adopted two children, Peter and Kate, and settled down after four years of moving around.

Mine had been a lucky war. I came out of it all in one piece, I was happily married, and I had spent much of the four years working at my civilian occupation. I had learned a lot about filmmaking during the war. I was soon promoted from assistant film editor to film editor and won an Academy Award for *Body and Soul*, the first feature film I actually edited.

In those days in Hollywood, the prevailing theory was that the cutting room was a good place to learn to become a director. The year after I won the Oscar, I was nominated again for editing *All the King's Men*. For three years I edited films for such top directors as Milestone, Cukor, and Ophuls. Finally I was offered a low-budget melodrama, *Cry Danger* starring Dick Powell, to direct.

I went to see my friend Billy Wilder for advice. He was one of the wisest and best directors in the business.

"This is my first directing job and I'm a bit nervous about it," I said. "You've made some of the best pictures ever made. Tell me anything that might be helpful."

"Start in the cutting room," said Billy.

"I already did that, Billy," I said.

He stood up and started to pace up and down. "Well, from then on there's not much to it," he said. "You just get yourself a script, a million bucks, some stars, a crew, a distributor, and you shoot the picture. Then you put it in rough cut and preview it in front of a live audience. Then you vomit, take the print back to the cutting room, and start to work."

I followed Billy's advice as closely as I could. *Cry Danger* got some good reviews. It was moderately successful at the box office and I was immoderately proud. I was a movie director, and that's what I had wanted to be since I was ten years old.

THE WORLD IS A BACK LOT

9

They're Only Making a Movie

After the war, the makers of Hollywood movies decided to venture forth from their sound stages and go out and see the world, as American soldiers, sailors, flyers, and Red Cross girls had been doing for four years. They discovered that motion picture audiences would no longer accept papier-mâché B-17's, cardboard destroyers, and plastic jungles after they had seen the real things.

In the 1950s the United States Congress passed a law that was later dubbed "the eighteen-month gravy train." It was originally intended to attract American oil workers to hardship areas. For example, if you helped build U.S. oil rigs in the hot, dry sands of Saudi Arabia or the cold, wet depths of the North Sea for eighteen months (without setting foot in the continental United States), you could keep whatever you earned, tax-free. It took a short time for motion-picture agents, lawyers, and business managers to hear about this loophole and an even shorter time for them to advise their clients to accept assignments abroad, if the pay was good and the assignments could be stretched out to eighteen months. Many highly paid motion-picture people listened to their advisers and hopped on the first available plane or luxury liner.

Quite often, American companies formed partnerships with foreign companies to take advantage of income from abroad that could pay for labor, transportation, and other production costs if the funds were actually disbursed in the foreign country. United Artists joined the J. Arthur Rank Organization to film H. E. Bates's novel *The Purple Plain*. Eric Ambler was signed to write the screenplay and I was signed to direct. The producer, John Bryan, was a producer who truly produced. He was also a brilliant designer—art director and a fine companion if you were trying to make a movie under difficult conditions. He was a tough infighter for everything he believed in. In 1952 he believed in *The Purple Plain*.

Bates wrote a colorful story about a British fighter pilot (Forrester) whose fiancée is killed in London during a German air raid. The pilot loses his will to live, is transferred to Burma, meets a beautiful Burmese girl (Anna), crashes his plane in the jungle, and realizes he would like to live after all, if he can get back to Anna and live with her. The odds are against his survival, but he fights his way through to her and safety and a happy ending. Eric Ambler kept close to the original story, but he made a number of improvements and came up with a fine script. All we needed was an opening sequence for the picture, but that could come later.

Among the many actors in Europe at the time of *The Purple Plain* were Clark Gable, Gene Kelly, Gregory Peck, and Bing Crosby. Of these, Gable or Peck would have been fine as RAF fighter pilots if they had had British accents, which they didn't, or we could change the leading man—pilot to a Canadian, which we did. One of the essential ingredients for a successful international coproduction was an American box-office star.

Gregory Peck was in Rome and had just finished starring in *Roman Holiday* for William Wyler. Audrey Hepburn was his co-star. Wyler came to London and I had dinner with him. He didn't mention *Dangerous Silence*. A gent all the way. I told him about the *Purple Plain* project and that, for the Burmese girl, we were considering Jennifer Jones, Gene Tierney, and other stars whose eyes could be "orientalized" with a bit of tape and a competent makeup artist.

"How are Audrey Hepburn's eyes?" I asked.

"Beautiful," said Willy.

"I mean, 'orientalwise,' " I said.

"Very wise, but not very oriental," said Willy. "Why don't you try to find a real Burmese girl?"

"Good idea," I said. "I'm going to Burma to look for locations next month. I'll keep a sharp lookout. What's it like working with Greg Peck?"

"Great. I know he wants to stay abroad for a few more months. Why don't you send him a script and go talk to him?"

Peck liked the script and agreed to do the picture under two conditions: (1) it must be shot on real locations in Southeast Asia, and (2) Anna must be played by a real Burmese, not some Hollywood actress with taped eyes.

"You've been talking with Willy," I said.

"He's made some fine pictures," said Greg. "I talk with him as much as I can." He smiled and I smiled and we shook hands.

One of the best parts of location filmmaking is the reconnaissance, or "recce," trip. That's when a few key people go out and do the all-important preproduction work. The director usually goes with the producer, production manager, art director, cameraman, assistant director, and, sometimes, an accountant. They cast extras and small parts, select locations, make arrangements with local people for lodging, transportation, and meals, and prepare countless other details necessary for smooth location work.

For *The Purple Plain* we flew to Rangoon before proceeding north to Myitkyina, where H. E. Bates had actually written the story. We set up an office in the Queens Hotel and I put an ad in the local paper: *Young Burmese actress wanted to play opposite Gregory Peck in United Artists–J. Arthur Rank film — Contact John Bryan or Robert Parrish — Queens Hotel.*

Shortly after the paper appeared on the streets, the manager of the hotel called our suite and said, "There are two hundred girls here to see you. Some are accompanied by relatives. It all adds up to over three hundred people in the lobby and on the street outside the hotel. Shall I send them up, or will you come down?"

"I'll come down," I said.

About half of the aspiring leading ladies were actually just aspiring to meet "Griggory Pick." When I told them he wasn't with us, they bowed politely and drifted away. John Bryan and I spent the next week interviewing girls of all types and sizes. Some were interesting, but none was interesting enough . . .

until Win Min Than arrived. First of all, she was beautiful. Some of the others were beautiful too, but Win had a certain quality, a presence, that John and I reacted to immediately. She spoke perfect English and was wearing a pale fawn native Burmese dress from her delicate throat to her delicate ankles, and she was carrying a sleek, blue-grey Burmese cat with eyes the same color as her dress. She was a knockout. The next day I shot several rolls of 16-mm color film of Win. She took direction very well and agreed to come to London for further tests.

John and I and the rest of the recce crew flew up to Myitkyina, selected our locations, completed our other work, and returned to London.

Two weeks later John Davis, the head of the Rank Organization, summoned John Bryan and me to his office on South Street and told us he was canceling the picture. He said that because of Communist activity on the China-Burma border, no insurance underwriters would insure Gregory Peck if the film was shot in Burma. Bryan and I exchanged glances, and then Bryan got to his feet and once again proved his qualifications as a producer.

"Then we'll shoot it somewhere else," he said.

"I've already notified United Artists," said Davis. He smiled, the way a rattlesnake smiles before he bites you. He had never been keen on *The Purple Plain.*

"Did you notify them that they will have to pay Peck and Parrish off, in dollars?" said Bryan. "They both have play-or-pay contracts."

"I'll negotiate that with their agents," smiled Davis.

"The Burmese leading lady is arriving next week for screen tests," said Bryan. "We're flying her in from Rangoon." He smiled back at Davis. "First class," he added.

Davis turned to me and said, "Will you excuse us, Bob?"

I said, "Certainly," and went back to my office and called my agent, Christopher Mann.

"Don't worry about it," said Chris. "They're in too deep to pull out. Besides, United Artists needs the picture, and Rank doesn't have the dollars to buy you and Peck out."

He was right. Davis "negotiated" with Christopher Mann and Peck's agent, Jack Dunfee. They both told him in polite negotiator's language to pay up or be sued. John Davis caved in and told John Bryan to proceed with the production.

Bryan started making plans for a new recce trip, and I went to Heathrow Airport to greet Win Min Than. She stepped off the plane carrying a giant stuffed leopard and another stuffed animal that I couldn't identify. She was beautiful in London, just as she had been in Rangoon. I put her up at a charming inn called The Bull at Gerrard's Cross, near Pinewood Studio, and we started testing the next day.

Geoffrey Unsworth, the camerman, pointed out that Win shook her head from side to side slightly whenever she spoke. This wasn't noticeable in medium and long shots, but in big close-ups it was disastrous. It made her look as though she had palsy. Every time she spoke, her head would shake and half of it would pop out of the frame. I asked Win if she could speak without shaking her head and she said no.

"Why not?" I asked.

"Because it's our way of showing approval," she said. "Western people nod their heads to show that they agree during a conversation. We shake ours. We've been doing it for hundreds of years, before Marco Polo, even. It's natural to us."

"Well, in a movie, it's not natural to have half of your face cut off every time you talk to someone," I said. "Let's try it again and see if you can keep your head still."

She made an honest effort, but she couldn't do it. Finally, the prop man made a brace like the old-fashioned photographers used. He added two sharp nails that touched her head behind her ears. Whenever she was in a close-up we strapped the brace on her, and after a while she stopped shaking her head every time she was punctured.

On our second recce trip, we went to Pakistan, India, Bangladesh, and Ceylon. We found a Burmese colony on Ceylon and decided to shoot there. The weather was perfect when the chartered BOAC plane arrived from London with the cast and crew. We had chosen the dry season because the script called for the pilot to almost die of thirst on his trek after the plane crash.

John Bryan had found two new Spitfires in Australia and had them flown in to an abandoned RAF airfield in the Ceylon jungle. He shipped a matching Spitfire in from Singapore, broke it up, and dragged it into a dry riverbed for the crash scenes. He built or found accommodations for over a hundred people deep in the jungle near Sigiriya Rock. The company arrived on a Wednesday, and the shooting was to start the following Monday.

On Thursday, John Bryan and I went to Colombo to meet the plane that was to bring Win Min Than from Rangoon. When she got out of the plane, she was accompanied by a short, bespectacled, smiling Burmese man. They both wore the traditional Burmese long skirts (*longyis*). "I want you to meet my husband, Jimmy," Win said. This was the first we had heard of him, but not the last. He stayed with us for the whole twelve weeks.

The day before we started shooting, the rains came and continued for eight solid days and nights, a proper monsoon. And the more it rained, the more the natives told us it was unseasonal, their heads shaking sincerely as they talked. The dry riverbed became a raging torrent and swept our wrecked Spitfire away the first night. Spirits fell, tempers rose, and John Bryan and his crew constructed some interior cover sets in one of the RAF hangars.

After this rough beginning, we felt we could overcome any obstacle. We finished our work at Sigiriya Rock and moved north to the bleak flatlands around Elephant Pass. The RAF provided fifty tents and furnished them as best they could with mosquito netting, lanterns, and two military cots each, and we moved in. My tentmate was Gregory Peck.

John Bryan arranged for breakfast to be served in the tents so that we could start shooting shortly after first light. We finished shooting two hours before sundown, had a delicious native-cooked meal, and were warned not to go outside after dark "because of the kraits." At first I thought "the kraits" might be some hostile, head-hunting savages, but they turned out to be extremely venomous nocturnal snakes that lurk in the Ceylonese jungle, hoping to sink their deadly fangs into any warm-blooded mammal that crosses their path, regardless of race, creed, or color. They are about the size of a pencil and usually lie in wait on low-hanging branches of trees.

During the shooting of *The Purple Plain*, Gregory Peck was

preoccupied with personal problems far from Ceylon. Most nights he would crawl onto his mosquito-netted cot, turn on his flashlight, and read. Some nights he would lie there on his back, staring at the ceiling of the tent. I would usually flop on my cot, say, "See you tomorrow," and sink into a dreamless sleep. From time to time, I would wake up at some odd hour and look over at Greg. He was always reading or staring. I never caught him sleeping.

One morning, at about 2:00, an ungodly scream woke me up. I saw Greg jump out of his cot, knock the center tent pole down, and disappear through the flaps of the front entrance, his mosquito net flowing behind him. I fought my way out of my mosquito net and the collapsed canvas and chased after him. He was screaming like a wounded $250,000-per-picture banshee and heading, barefooted, for the jungle, the kraits, and the end of a $2-million British-American coproduction. I ran faster and yelled "Greg!" a couple of times, but that seemed to speed him up even more. He tripped on the mosquito netting, got up, and plunged on.

At the edge of the compound I caught up with him and tackled him. I tackled Gregory Peck, one of the most famous movie stars in the world.

"Are you all right?" I asked. He stared at me, dead-eyed, then put both hands over his face and gasped for breath.

"Are you all right, Greg?" I asked again.

After what seemed like a very long time, he took his hands away from his face and said quietly, "I'm fine."

"Well," I said, "would you like to come back and help me rebuild our tent so we can get some sleep before we start shooting four hours from now?"

He nodded his handsome head and said, "I'd like that very much."

I helped him to his bare feet and led him back to our tent. We put the tent pole up and crawled onto our cots. Greg said, "Some kind of nightmare, I guess," and went right to sleep. I lay there, wide awake, thinking. When our breakfast arrived at 5:00, I went over and shook Greg awake.

"How do you feel?" I said.

"Fine," said Greg. "Why?"

"Do you remember what went on here last night?" I asked.

"More or less," he said, and smiled his shy, expensive smile.

"Do you mind if we use it for the opening scene in the picture?" I said.

"Be my guest," said our gracious star, still smiling.

Two nights later we shot the scene with an RAF crewman called Nobby playing my part. We got it all in one take. I guess that's because Greg and I had rehearsed it so well.

After that, things went relatively smoothly. We kept on our schedule and faced our last day of shooting with enthusiasm. The end was in sight. Our last shot was a close-up of Win Min Than when Peck staggers out of the jungle after his trek and takes her in his arms for the first time. The actors were made up, Win's anti-head-shaking brace was strapped into position, and we rehearsed the scene up to the point where Peck is supposed to kiss the Burmese beauty. I wanted to save the actual kiss for the actual take and, I hoped, get it the first time.

We were finally ready to shoot. Peck and Win stepped out from in front of the camera for final makeup adjustments. Win's husband, Jimmy, patted Win's hand affectionately.

When the actors were back in position and I said, "OK, let's go," Geoff Unsworth held up his hand and asked me to look through the camera. As I put my eye to the lens, he whispered, "Look at Win's left cheek." I did. It was puffed out as though she had the mumps. As I watched, the lump changed to the right cheek. She obviously had chewing gum or chewing tobacco or something in her mouth. I went to her like a schoolmaster to a naughty pupil. I put my hand in front of her mouth and said, "Give it to me." She looked over at her husband, Jimmy. He shook his head. Win closed her lips tightly.

"All right, let's take a break," I said.

I loosened the nail brace behind Win's ears, took her by the hand, and walked her over to Jimmy.

"What the hell is going on?" I said.

Jimmy grinned. Win started to giggle uncontrollably and a clove of garlic popped out of her mouth. It turned out that Jimmy was jealous of Peck and insisted that Win chew some garlic before and during any kissing scenes with Peck.

I called lunch. John Bryan took Jimmy by the arm and led him off into the jungle, and I never saw him again. The com-

David Lean and Sam Spiegel hold a story conference in the
desert on the set of *Lawrence of Arabia,* Jordan, 1961.

Sam Spiegel aboard the *Malahne*, Monte Carlo, 1961.

Sam Spiegel and Marie-Helèna Arnaud aboard the *Malahne*.

Mas de l'Horizon
Année 1973
Sam Spiegel

Personalized label for the wine served on the *Malahne.*

Sam Spiegel with Marie-Helèna Arnaud and Kathie Parrish
aboard the *Malahne,* Cadaqués, Spain, 1961.

Sam with son Adam, Hyde Park, London, 1968.

Sam in Hyde Park.

Adam and Sam Spiegel with author, London, 1976.

Adam and Sam Spiegel, London, 1976.

Kathie, Bob, Kate, and Peter Parrish with beagle, Timmy, Los Angeles, 1958.

Cinematographer Gregg Toland shows OSS film crew the ropes,
Washington, DC, 1942.

Author greeting Win Min Than, Heathrow Airport, London, 1953.

Author and Gregory Peck, *The Purple Plain*, Ceylon, 1953.

Gregory Peck and Lyndon Brook, *The Purple Plain.*

Gregory Peck and Win Min Than, *The Purple Plain*.

Hotel Chesa Grischuna, Klosters, Switzerland.

Rita Hayworth and visitor Ingrid Bergman on the set of *Fire Down Below*, London, 1956.

Jack Lemmon, Edric Connor, Robert Mitchum, and author,
Fire Down Below, Tobago, 1956.

Joanne Dru, Richard Widmark, author, and visitors Joel and Jody McCrea, *My Pal Gus*, Twentieth Century–Fox studio, Los Angeles, 1952.

pany nurse provided a mint-flavored spray for Win. Peck, always a gentleman, watched everything with bemused silence.

After lunch, we rehearsed once and were halfway through shooting the scene when two plump American lady tourists appeared out of nowhere and stepped in front of the camera with autograph books. They charged up to Peck and asked for his autograph. I yelled, "Cut!" and Peck, one of the most patient actors I've ever worked with, turned away from Win Min Than and said sharply, "I'll sign your books later. We're working now."

The two ladies were stunned. Their jaws dropped, they looked at each other for a moment, then they retreated. As they passed the camera, where I was standing, one of them said indignantly, "Working! They're only making a movie!"

One year later, when John Davis escorted the queen of England to the Royal Command Performance of *The Purple Plain* at the Empire Cinema in Piccadilly Circus, he was smiling, just as he had smiled when he'd tried to cancel the picture.

C. A. Lejeune, the highly respected film critic for *The Observer*, wrote, "H. E. Bates has been well served. Gregory Peck gives one of his best performances and Win Min Than, his beautiful Burmese co-star, is delightful. She has the talent of stillness."

When I read the review, I thought of the sharp nails behind Win's delicate Burmese ears.

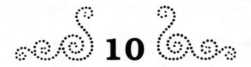

10

Klosters

If you ever spend two years preparing, shooting, and editing a film in Ceylon and want somewhere to recuperate, I can't think of a better place than Klosters, Switzerland.

My two friends Peter Viertel and Irwin Shaw discovered Klosters before I did. We had met during the war and cemented our friendship in Hollywood, and when they told me how good the skiing was in Klosters, I hurried on over with Kathie and our children.

We stayed at the Chesa Grischuna, a charming hotel in the center of the small, picture-postcard village. We skied every day on some of the most beautiful runs in the world, we dined on some of the best meals, we met some of the most interesting people, and, at the end of our two-week holiday, we were hooked. We impulsively took a long lease on a chalet across the street from the Chesa Grischuna. It was one of the best impulses we ever had. A holiday home away from our London home.

11

Hemingway
and
How to Write for the Movies
(Part I)

I met Ernest Hemingway twice, once in 1953 and again in 1956, both times at the Chantaco Hotel in the Basque country, just outside St.-Jean-de-Luz. The first time we met, I knew who he was but he didn't know who I was. That was before I directed a movie in Tobago with a script by Irwin Shaw and starring Rita Hayworth, Jack Lemmon, and Robert Mitchum.

When we met again three years later, the movie had been released and Ernest Hemingway still didn't know who I was, but I still knew who he was. I state this right out so that the reader won't be misled into thinking that this is another of the rash of Hemingway-was-my-best-friend stories that keep popping up since the famous writer blew his brains out with a shotgun in Ketchum, Idaho, on July 2, 1961.

Most of these professional Hemingway-knowers of varying nationalities, talents, and moralities knew Hemingway better than I did. I won't try to compete with their learned accounts of the great man's work, nor will I attempt to assess his unique contribution to American writing. The Swedish Academy summed it up when Hemingway was awarded the Nobel Prize:

> For his powerful style-forming mastery of the art of modern narration, as most recently evinced in *The Old Man and the Sea*. . . . Hemingway's earlier writings displayed brutal, cynical and callous signs which may be considered at variance with the

Nobel Prize requirements for a work of ideal ten-
dencies. But on the other hand he also possesses a
heroic pathos which forms the basic element of his
awareness of life, a manly love of danger and adventure, with a natural admiration of every individual
who fights the good fight in a world of reality over-
shadowed by violence and death.

So this story is not so much about Ernest Hemingway,
whom I knew for such a short time, but is, like the rest of this
book, mostly about the movies. It just happens that my two
brief meetings with this legendary writer will help me tell my
story.

In July 1953 Ernest Hemingway agreed to return to Spain
for the first time since the Spanish Civil War. He had been
living in Cuba for fifteen years and had said he would not set
foot in Spain as long as any of his Spanish friends was still in
prison. When the Franco government decided to liberalize its
image and invited "artists and intellectuals" to return to
Spain, Picasso, Casals, and others declined, but the word was
quietly passed to Hemingway that his friends were no longer
in prison and he agreed to come back.

The Old Man and the Sea had been published the year
before, first in *Life* magazine, then by Scribner's, and was a
great success. After the unsatisfactory reception of his previous book, *Across the River and into the Trees,* Hemingway
was again riding high and felt that this would be the right time
to return to his beloved Spain.

He said that one of the reasons for his return was to introduce his fourth wife, Mary, to the Feria de San Fermín in
Pamplona, about which he had written in *The Sun Also Rises.*
There were other reasons, not the least of which was that he
loved Spain and the Spanish people with a passion matched
only by his passion for writing, hunting, fishing, bravery, loy-
alty, men, women, motor cars, bullfighting, good wine, and all
of the other things that so many Hemingway scholars have
written about.

My friend Peter Viertel was responsible for my meeting
Hemingway. Peter was a friend and respecter of Hemingway,
but I was only a respecter. I had read his work and admired

most of it, but I had a vague feeling that it would be better to know him through his writing than in person. Peter had asked me and my wife, Kathie, to meet him and his wife, Jigee, at the Chantaco Hotel. He said we would join the Hemingways there and drive to Pamplona together.

The Chantaco is one of those places you want to go back to whether Ernest Hemingway and Peter Viertel are there or not. It is a low, white, rambling Spanish type of building surrounded by a deep-green golf course and dripping with bougainvillea. There are six blossom-bearing orange trees in the patio, and when you sit with your back to the hotel lobby, you can see three tennis courts through the arch on the left of the patio. Rene Lacoste, the famous French Davis Cup player, was in charge of the tennis courts at the time.

I had my car, an Austin A-40 convertible, full out and was a hundred yards past the hotel entrance when Kathie said, "There it is. You passed it." I slammed on the brakes, started to back up, then realized that my wife had turned the rearview mirror in her direction.

She said, "Ohmygod, I look terrible."

I turned around and drove back to the Chantaco.

The parking area is next to the patio, and as I turned off the ignition, I saw Ernest Hemingway and Jigee Viertel sitting under the orange trees with a bottle of white wine in an ice bucket between them, their backs to us. Even from this angle, Jigee looked cool and fresh and beautiful and Hemingway looked cool and noble and famous. A soft breeze carried the scent of the orange blossoms to the parking area, where Kathie and I were now sweatily unsticking ourselves from the plastic seats of the A-40 convertible and trying to keep out of sight long enough for Kathie to get a scarf over her head, put on some lipstick, fix her eyes, adjust her bra, hitch her girdle, pull down her skirt, put her shoes on, spray under her arms, fix her purse, and hiss "Don't hurry me" several times. I know how long these little things can take, so I decided to put the top up to cover for her. At the crucial moment, the point of no return, the moment when you give the extra hitch and get the top up or chicken out and let it drop again, my wife whispered, "Have you seen my scarf?" I turned around to say something witty or sarcastic or preferably both, but she wasn't there. I twisted around farther, holding the top with one hand now, and spotted her crouched under the dashboard fixing her makeup. Before I could come up with the right comment, the top collapsed and caught my right thumb. I yelled "For Christ's sakes" or "Oh, shit" or something and heard Jigee say, "Here they are now."

When I had freed my thumb, I looked up and saw Jigee walking toward us. Her peaches-and-cream complexion was as luminous as ever, and she was smiling her usual devastating smile.

"Welcome to Basqueland," she said. "Where's Kathie?"

"She's under the dashboard," I said. "Can you get me a Band-Aid?"

She looked at my thumb, which was now bleeding a bit, not much, and said, "How in Christ's name did you do that?"

I said, "I mashed it looking for Kathie's scarf."

Kathie now came out from under cover, looking like a million dollars. In a few seconds she had somehow miraculously transformed herself from a sweaty pain in the neck to a stunning beauty wearing dark glasses, that fuchsia lipstick that was popular then, and a Hermes scarf over her head. She jumped up on the seat looking like a TV commercial and greeted her friend Jigee enthusiastically. They both told each other that they looked great, the way people do whether they look great or not, and Jigee said, "Come meet Papa."

I was now sucking my thumb and feeling sorry for myself, but I wasn't getting any sympathy from the two girls and thought it would be a mistake to meet the man who wrote *Death in the Afternoon* with my thumb in my mouth, so I curled it into my fingers and followed along to the table where Hemingway was now standing.

He was impressive, all right, a star, the way Churchill and Garbo and Franklin D. Roosevelt were stars. I guess his head was the first thing I noticed, that and the large, round belly, which he later told Kathie was made not of fat but of muscles that had "dropped down to a more comfortable position." A wide old leather belt held up a pair of unpressed grey trousers that hung loosely around his thin hips. A short whitish-grey beard covered a skin rash, which he scratched from time to time. Above his left eye there was a large welt from some ancient wound, and I noticed that his left elbow was scarred and a different shape from his right elbow. He had sea-green, brownish eyes with rings of little trout-specks around the outsides of the irises. He looked straight at me, but because of the legend, I thought he was looking through me. Everything about him was awesome, romantic, larger than life. Except his shyness.

When Jigee introduced Kathie, he rubbed his beard, lowered his eyes, shifted from one foot to the other, and muttered something that I wish I could have understood. Then Jigee said, "And this is Bob." He suddenly became unshy. He thrust out his big, hairy right hand and focused his strong eyes on my weak ones and said, "I'm glad to meet you, Bob." His eyes were good and true and straight, the same as Robert Jordan's in *For Whom the Bell Tolls*. I knew we were in the Basque country, but I also knew a Midwestern twang when I heard one. I put my hand out, forgetting that my fingers were still wrapped around my throbbing thumb. Hemingway grasped my clubbed fist and squeezed it as though he knew it was probably an old war wound and was too fine to make anything of it except to mash it, hard.

Jigee went into the hotel to tell Peter and Mary Hemingway that we had arrived. Hemingway asked Kathie and me to sit down, and then he poured some white wine for both of us. He looked at Kathie over his glass and said, "Good luck, daughter." From then on Hemingway had her eating out of his marvelous big, callused hands (callused from typing? skinning buffalo? cleaning elephant guns? wrestling with sharks? caressing Lady Brett? what?). He was kind, gentle, eager to please — everything I feared he would not be. He was particularly charming with the ladies. He called Jigee and Kathie daughter. He called his wife Miss Mary and she called him Ernest, and when he walked faster than she could walk, she ran.

Hemingway said, "Miss Mary has taken up photography, that's why she will have three cameras hanging around her neck. In short time has become one of the best photographers, except maybe Capa . . . one or two others." I had read that he often talked in a kind of shorthand, leaving out certain words, usually personal pronouns and articles. He turned to me and said, "Pete tells me you crossed the Rhine with Capa in nineteen forty-five."

I said, "Yes, well, we didn't actually cross together. I was a navy photographer attached to the Ninth Armored Division at Remagen, and Capa parachuted in behind the German lines, on the other side of the river."

"But you knew him," said Hemingway.

"Yes," I said. "We knew each other. Capa took great pictures of the operation and they were published in *Life* magazine and seen by millions of people, and I took some pictures that were only seen by the U.S. Navy lab technicians in Paris."

Hemingway glanced at Kathie and said, "Daughter, did you ever know Capa?" Kathie said she had met him in Hollywood after the war when he had played a bit part in a movie. Hemingway said he didn't think Capa had ever been an actor. He seemed to be challenging Kathie, so I said, "Yes, he played an Arab named Hamza in a movie called *Temptation*. It was directed by Irving Pichel. Merle Oberon, George Brent, Charles Korvin, and Paul Lukas were the stars."

Hemingway turned his eyes back to me, and I remembered that Gertrude Stein had written, "He was rather foreign-looking, with passionately interested, rather than interesting, eyes." I was thinking about this when Hemingway said, "Why?"

"Why what?" I answered.

He sipped his white wine and said, "That's a Basque wine. It's not French and it's not Spanish and it's clean and it's fresh and it's true."

I raised my glass to my lips and took a deep gulp. "Yes," I said, "it's very true."

He settled back and said, "Why were Capa's pictures better than yours?"

I took another sip of the Basque wine and said, "You're right, it's not only true, it's clean."

"What's clean?" he said.

"The wine. This Basque wine. It's true and clean."

He put his glass down and studied me. "What about Capa?" he said.

"He came up to my cutting room at Universal Studio in his

thick pancake makeup and his eyeshadow and his Arab djel-
laba and —"

"Wasn't asking about Capa the actor," Hemingway said.
"Interested in Capa the photographer."

"Oh," I said. "Well, after the Remagen Bridge collapsed, I
came back to Paris and turned my negatives in to Adm. Kirk's
office, and then I went over to the Scribe Hotel and bumped
into Capa at the bar. This was only two weeks after the Rhine
crossing, and Capa's pictures were already printed in *Life*
magazine."

Hemingway swallowed the last of his wine and called the
waiter. "Bring us another bottle of *vin Basque*," he said.

"As you know," I said, "Capa always looked sleepy, and it
was hard to figure out when he *did* anything. I understood
how he jumped out of an airplane at night and took the pictures at first light, but I couldn't figure out how he got them to
Paris and had them processed and into *Life* magazine before
my negatives were even developed. I knew his pictures were
better than mine, and I was anxious to find out why."

"I hope you didn't ask him," said Hemingway.

"Yes, I did," I said.

The waiter brought the new bottle of wine and filled the
glasses. Hemingway sipped his and said, "Let me see the
bottle." The waiter showed it to him and Hemingway said,
"That will do fine." There was no label on the bottle.

I felt that I had trespassed too far into Capa-Hemingway
territory and was relieved at the waiter's interruption. I
thought if I could switch the conversation to wine, I wouldn't
have to say anything about Capa that Hemingway would dis-
approve of.

"This doesn't taste like the other bottle," I said.

"What did Capa say when you asked him about how to take
pictures?"

"It seems drier, flintier, more like a Sancerre," I stalled.

Hemingway put his glass down. "Would be interested to
hear anything Capa had to say about taking pictures. Never
talked about it much to me."

My mind went back ten years to the Scribe Bar. The room
was crowded with U.S. military personnel, journalists, and a

sprinkling of British, French, Belgian, and Dutch officers.
Capa leaned back, looking half-asleep, a cigarette hanging out
of the corner of his mouth. He had ordered a bottle of Bisquit
Dubouché cognac and we had both had three drinks. It was
the first time I had heard of Bisquit Dubouché cognac.

"Tell me about taking pictures," I said. "What's the secret?"

"Take a lot," said Capa.

"I did."

"How many?"

"As many as I could under the circumstances. The light was
lousy on the Rhine, and it takes time to set the exposure, focus,
and compose your picture. Even so, I must have brought back
several hundred negatives."

"Not enough," Capa said. "First of all, you shouldn't waste
time trying for perfect composition. Let the lab do that. Every
lab has at least one genius. You find out who that is and you
dump your negatives on him. Then you trust him. You also
love him, treasure him, bribe him, cajole him, beg him. 'Do
the best you can,' you plead. 'Bring up the shadows, underde-
velop the hot sections, crop out the dull parts, make me look
good. I'm giving you a thousand negatives. *Life* magazine only
needs twenty. The law of averages will help, but if you pick
out the *best* sections of those twenty law-of-averages photos,
you'll make me a hero.' Then you find a case of Moët et Chan-
don champagne, have it delivered to this genius in the lab
before your negatives go into the bath." Capa looked around
the room and spotted a beautiful American Red Cross girl
sitting alone.

"Take care of the bill," he said. "I'll settle with you later."
He took his glass of brandy and headed for the Red Cross girl.
Before he reached her, an American colonel arrived at her
table. She stood up and kissed the colonel warmly. Capa
stopped and watched the tender scene for a moment, and
when the girl looked over at him, he raised his glass in a silent
toast, bowed politely, and returned to the bar. "After the negatives come out," he said, "you go in and help the lab genius
drink the champagne."

Hemingway said, "You're saying Capa's pictures were
made in the lab. Is that what you're saying?"

I sipped my flinty Basque wine, wishing Capa had never told me anything about photography, wishing I were somewhere else, wishing I had never met Hemingway, who I felt was trying to trap me into saying that Capa was a sniveling coward and a bad photographer as well.

"I was just repeating what Capa told me," I said.

"Did he tell you that he was one of the bravest men I ever met?" said Hemingway.

"Well, no," I said. "We didn't talk much about bravery. We talked mostly about photography and girls and horse racing and things like that."

I knew I had made a bad start and had talked too much, and I was glad when Peter Viertel and Jigee and Mary Hemingway came out before I blabbed even more. As Hemingway had predicted, Mary had three cameras around her neck, and after Peter introduced her to Kathie and me, she took some pictures of us.

Mary was an attractive, intense woman who looked after her husband with a devotion that was touching. During the next four days, Hemingway was seldom out of her sight and quite often in her lens. She had very expensive photographic equipment, and she took so many pictures that I thought maybe she was another pupil of Capa's. She was warm and polite to Jigee and Kathie, warmer to Peter and me, and warmest to Hemingway. It was apparent from the moment I first saw them together that they needed and appreciated each other.

The Hemingways had a Lancia and an Italian chauffeur named Adamo. Peter and Jigee had a sporty little MG, which Peter kept tuned like a Swiss watch. He had a Swiss watch too, a Rolex, with a hand-tooled leather strap and a silver buckle. He looked at it and said, "We'd better hit the road if we want to be in Pamplona before dark." We piled into the cars and headed for the Spanish border.

The French authorities waved us through, but the Spaniards stopped us and asked for all our passports. I had never been to Spain, and this seemed normal procedure to me. However, Hemingway appeared nervous and called Peter aside for consultation. I walked over to join them, thinking I was a member of the team, but Hemingway stopped talking as I approached. The polite immigration officer returned our passports without comment, and this seemed to disappoint Hemingway. He showed his passport to the immigration officer a second time and the man pointed out that it had already been stamped.

The customs official had been going through our bags, and when they opened a small canvas bag of Hemingway's, there was a copy of *For Whom the Bell Tolls,* the book for which Hemingway had been banned from Spain. I had read in *Vogue* magazine that he was one of those rare "men who make things happen," and I feared that what he'd make happen here would be to get himself and his pals thrown into a Spanish jail.

I needn't have worried. The customs man glanced at the book as if it were a Michelin guide or the Old Testament. He paid no attention to it whatsoever. Hemingway reached over and kind of slid it into his sightline, but the man simply was not interested. He rummaged through the Viyella shirts and baseball caps (from Abercrombie and Fitch) and closed the bag. The Guardia Civil stood around in their three-cornered patent-leather hats with rifles strapped across their backs and smiled as though we were all German tourists. Hemingway finally shook hands with one of the Guardia Civil officers and off we went to the Feria de San Fermín at Pamplona.

"He's darling," said my wife as we followed Peter's MG through a beautiful canyon beside a turbulent mountain stream. The Hemingways and Adamo brought up the rear in the Lancia.

"Who?" I asked, knowing full well that she didn't mean the customs man, the immigration man, the Guardia Civil, Peter Viertel, or me or Adamo, who Hemingway had confided was an undertaker when he wasn't chauffeuring.

"Ernest Hemingway," she said. "Papa." I knew that lots of people called him Papa, but we had only known him a few hours and it seemed presumptuous to me to adopt this affectionate nickname so early in the relationship.

"Why do you call him Papa?" I asked.

"Why not?" said my wife. "He calls me daughter, and besides, he told me I could call him Papa." She adjusted the rearview mirror so that she could see his car following us.

"He calls all wives daughter," I said. I adjusted the mirror back, so that *I* could see the car following us. Hemingway was in the front seat with Adamo. Mary was in the back seat taking pictures through the window. Hemingway seemed to be sleeping.

"You don't like Ernest Hemingway, do you?" said my wife.

"Of course I like him. What makes you say a dumb thing like that?"

"I don't know. You seem to resent my calling him Papa the way everyone else does."

"I don't call him Papa."

"No, but you talked his ear off. Why did you have to tell him all that dumb war stuff about Capa? Jesus, I thought you'd never stop talking."

I had thought I wouldn't either, but I wasn't going to tell her that. Instead I pointed out some armed Guardia Civil soldiers who were stationed at each end of a bridge we were approaching. "Look at that," I said. "Every bridge guarded as though someone might blow it up."

By now Kathie was on one of her favorite themes and wasn't going to be diverted by any small talk about Spanish bridges. "Why do men your age feel compelled to flaunt your foxhole time when you meet Ernest Hemingway?" she said. "Don't you think he gets fed up with the horrors of war?"

"He asked me about Bob Capa and I told him about Bob Capa." We were on the bridge now and I said, "I wonder if this is the bridge he wrote about in *For Whom the Bell Tolls*."

"No," she said. "That one was in the mountains near Madrid, up around Avila and Segovia. Didn't you read the book?"

"Of course I did. It was about the Spanish Civil War, and Capa was with Hemingway in the Spanish Civil War, and that's why Hemingway was interested in Capa, and that's why he asked me about Capa, and that's why I told him about Capa." I snapped the radio on but it was a news broadcast in Spanish, which neither of us understood, so I snapped it off. We drove in silence for about five minutes.

"You told him more about Capa than he wanted to know," she said finally.

I drove on, pretending that the mountain roads demanded my full attention.

"Imagine telling Ernest Hemingway about how tough it

was in the trenches," she said. "Jesus Christ, Foxhole Charlie
and the Hundred Years' War."

I shifted down into third gear, then second, then abortively
tried to jam the A-40 into low gear, forgetting where it was on
the goddamn English car. I glanced in the mirror. Hemingway's head had toppled over onto Adamo's shoulder. I wondered if he had ever told any of *his* wives about *his* war experiences. Then I thought, He doesn't have to. They can read
about them in his books.

We stopped for dinner at the Hotel Lecumberri, north of
Pamplona. The Hemingways were going to stay there and
Peter was to take the rest of us to a hotel on the Plaza de la
Constitution in the center of Pamplona. The proprietor and
most of the other people at the Lecumberri knew Hemingway
and were tearfully glad to see him. He spoke Spanish to them
and English to us, and he was gentle and kindly and helpful to
all. At dinner he told us about the Spanish wine we were
drinking ("From the Rioja district of Castille, watered by the
River Oja, a tributary of the Ebro"), the bullfights that would
start the next day, and how he would get the best tickets for us
from Juanito Quintana, his oldest and best Spanish friend,
who had introduced him to the sacred rites of bullfighting
when he attended his first San Fermín *feria* in 1922.

Juanito Quintana had been impresario of the Pamplona bull
ring and a successful hotel owner before the Civil War. He
was a Basque whose sympathies had been, and probably still
were, against the Franco regime; consequently he was no
longer an impresario and no longer a hotel owner, but he was
still a fine Basque gentleman, and Hemingway was sure he
wouldn't let us down with the tickets.

That night at the Lecumberri we saw Hemingway at his
best, teaching something he knew well to interested pupils.
His patience in answering our questions about the *feria* of San
Fermín was remarkable. Peter talked a little bit, but Kathie
and Jigee and I just sat and listened and admired and felt
lucky to be included in Hemingway's historic return to Spain.
Mary Hemingway was dignified and quiet. I suspected she
was familiar with most of what her husband was saying, but
she didn't nudge him or glare at him or say, "It's all in your

books, dear." She just beamed as though it was all as exciting and new to her as it was to us.

He still talked a lot in that strange Hemingway shorthand, but on some stories he talked along just the way he wrote, using personal pronouns, articles, verbs, and adjectives. He told us about a Cuban fishing trip on his boat, the *Pilar*. It seems that a fellow had come down to Havana to try to get Hemingway to write an article for an American magazine. Hemingway said he didn't want to write the article, so he took the fellow out on the *Pilar*, showed him some rough sea and some tuna blood on the deck, and the fellow took the next plane back to New York and never mentioned the magazine article again.

He said that a college professor had written a book about him in which it was decided that all of Hemingway's writing was the result of a trauma (he pronounced it "trowmah") that Hemingway had experienced when he was a boy. He said the only real "trowmah" he could remember having was when he had read the professor's book. He said he couldn't understand anyone writing a book about someone without meeting him, especially if the subject of the book was still alive. He said he wouldn't consider writing a book about the college professor, dead or alive, whether he had had a "trowmah" or not.

Then he told us about a baseball game in Chicago, a ski run and a pheasant shoot in Picabo, Idaho, and a war in France, in which he had "liberated" the Ritz Bar in Paris. Kathie glanced at me when he came to the part about meeting Bob Capa at the Ritz Bar, and I lowered my eyes demurely.

He then told us that he had formed a partnership with two pals, Leland Hayward and Spencer Tracy, and that they planned to make a movie from Hemingway's novel *The Old Man and the Sea*. He asked Peter if he would write the screenplay, but Peter said he didn't think he should.

"Why not?" said Hemingway.

"First of all, *The Old Man and the Sea* is a classic and I'm not sure it should be filmed," Peter said. Hemingway settled down and concentrated on every word. "To make it work as a movie," Peter went on, "the screenwriter would have to invent scenes that are not in the book. This would be presumptuous and probably completely unsatisfactory because it wouldn't be your work, it would be someone else's."

"Then you won't do it?" Hemingway said.

"I didn't say I wouldn't do it," Peter said. "I'm just pointing out some of the problems."

"Well, Pete, I said I would do this movie with Leland and Spence, and I'm not going back on my word. I need you because I think you are the best writer for the job."

Jigee said, "Papa, why are you getting involved in making a movie?"

He turned his big head to Jigee. You could tell from the way he looked at her that he was truly fond of her. Finally he said, "Why not?"

Jigee said, "I don't know. I just thought you were not interested in movies, especially when they're from your books. You didn't have anything to do with *Men Without Women*."

"Paid me five hundred dollars for the title," said Hemingway, "and then they had somebody named McGuinness write a story about a disabled submarine which had nothing to do with my short story collection. Spelled his name with two *n*'s and two *s*'s."

"What about *A Farewell to Arms*?"

"What about it?"

"You stated publicly that you had nothing to do with it. You once even advised a young writer to stay completely away from the movies."

"Where did you hear that?" he said.

"I heard it," said Jigee. Hemingway opened another bottle of Rioja and filled our glasses. "Young writer asked me, 'How do you write for the movies?' " He sipped his wine and ate three shrimps, heads and all. "Said, 'First you write it. Alone. Don't talk to anyone about it and don't let anyone see what you are writing, except maybe your wife if you're one of those *"well, I had to talk to somebody"* writers. Jews have a word for writer-helpers. Call them *kibitzers*. But Jews don't have a corner on these well-meaning folk. Gentiles have them too. Call them *collaborators* or *editors* or *critics* or *agents* or *parasites*. They're the chaps who say, *You write it and then we'll go over it*. If you have any talent, avoid them like the plague.' "

Peter spoke to the waiter in Spanish and the waiter brought a bowl of spicy chili peppers and some olives. Hemingway ate four more shrimps, one at a time, each followed by a gulp of red wine. He held out a pepper to Mary, one to Jigee, and one to Kathie. They each snapped them up like trained seals and tears began to cascade down their pretty cheeks, especially Jigee's.

Hemingway went on, "I told him, 'After you've written it and it's published and successfully reviewed, you get in a Stutz Bearcat or some other car that you can put the top down on, and drive west to the California border. When you reach the state line, turn left and drive south on the Arizona side until you get opposite Hollywood. Then shift down into low gear and fling the manuscript in. . . .' " He took a mouthful of wine and a handful of chili peppers and some shrimp and rolled them around in his wiskered jaws. He looked off into space, reflecting on something. Then he swallowed and said, "No, that's wrong. You don't throw the manuscript in until somebody throws some money out. As soon as you get the money counted, you lob the manuscript in with your left hand, the way you throw a grenade, and you shift into second, gun the motor, and head south, east, or north. Under no circumstances should you turn right. If you cross the state line and actually arrive in Hollywood, in person, you are finished as a writer."

A silence fell over the room and I looked at Peter, who had written some good novels and some good screenplays, the latter sometimes with collaborators. He had crossed the California state line many times and was not finished as a writer. He stared at his friend Hemingway and Hemingway stared back at him. I stared at the two of them, and the three ladies picked up their wineglasses at exactly the same time, as though they were in a movie scene and the director had just yelled, "Action!" After a while I lowered my eyes to the stone floor at the Lecumberri. The stones were about a foot square with dirt between, and while I was deciding whether the dirt patches were one inch or one-half inch wide, I heard Ernest Hemingway say, "Pete, asking as personal favor. Need you to write this screenplay. Will you do it?"

I looked up from the floor and heard my friend say, "Of course I'll do it, Papa."

The Feria de San Fermín started the next day. Most of the Hemingway-knowers have written about the *feria* and they've written about themselves and they've written about Hemingway writing about the *feria*. They have sat at the Cafe Choko under the wide arcades that run around the Plaza de la Constitution, and they have heard the rocket bombs explode at noon and watched the square fill up with men and boys dressed in white with red scarves around their necks, all dancing to the ancient Basque *riau-riau* music and singing along with the drum, fife, and reed instruments. Some have run through the streets of Pamplona with the bulls that are released each morning from the corrals at the Puerta Rochapea for the day's corrida. In their stories they usually call Hemingway Papa or Ernesto, and if they weren't running with the bulls, they wrote about watching the sport with Hemingway from his favorite spot on one of the steep, narrow streets of the town, sharing rough Spanish wine from goatskin botas with the *Pamplonistas*. They all seem to wind up at the Cafe Marcelino indulging in an orgy of Navarre culinary specialties supplied by the owner, Matias, a fellow who had befriended Hemingway when he was an unknown reporter and didn't know any more about bullfighting than I did. That is, Hemingway didn't know anything about it then. Matias always did.

It was on our trip to Pamplona that Hemingway first saw the matador Antonio Ordóñez in a corrida. Ordóñez's father, Cayetano Ordóñez, had been a leading bullfighter when Hemingway first came to Spain. Cayetano fought under the name of Niño de Palma; he had been the model for Hemingway's bullfighter Pedro Romero in *The Sun Also Rises*. Hemingway later decided that Ordóñez, Sr., was a coward. (A conclusion, strangely enough, reached about Hemingway by Gertrude Stein and William Faulkner. Stein: "He's yellow . . . just like the flatboat men on the Mississippi as described by Mark Twain." Faulkner, like Hemingway, a Nobel Prize winner: "Never out on a limb — never uses words that you have to stop reading to look up. Literary coward.")

Be that as it may, Hemingway saw Antonio Ordóñez perform and decided that Ordóñez would probably become the best bullfighter in the world. After the corrida, Hemingway went to the Hotel Yoldi and met Ordóñez. The history of their relationship for the next few years is recorded in several Hemingway-knower books, all more or less accurate, all claiming to have the only true facts. One of these literary gentlemen, a Spaniard, hints that Hemingway's obsession with Antonio Ordóñez had homosexual overtones. Another, an American this time, alleges that Hemingway actually said to him that "undeclared fairies follow bullfighters." In any event, it was at the Feria de San Fermín in Pamplona in 1953 that Hemingway met and attached himself to the son of Cayetano Ordóñez, a close friendship that lasted until Hemingway's death.

On the first day of the *feria*, after we had watched the running of the bulls, Mary Hemingway wanted to take pictures, and Hemingway suggested going to the horse fair where Navarre gypsies gathered to trade horses. He obviously loved Pamplona and was proud to pass his knowledge of its history along to his five attentive tourists, who were visiting the ancient city for the first time.

"Cathedral was built by Philip III, now buried inside the walls," said Hemingway. "Choir stalls carved in English oak by Miguel Ancheta. Ventura Rodriguez designed outside in 1783 and when he finished, started work on the aqueduct which still supplies Pamplona with water from Monte Francoa, nine miles away." He made it all interesting, as though Ventura Rodriguez were still alive and would start another project as soon as he wrapped up the aqueduct job. Mary took pictures, Peter and I asked questions, and Kathie and Jigee stared at Hemingway through their sunglasses.

We came to an ancient wall behind which the gypsies had tethered their horses. Mary said she wanted to take a group photo, and while she was reloading her Hasselblad and her Nikon and her Leica, Hemingway again told us how proud he was that Miss Mary had become such an expert photographer in such a short time. He praised her newfound talent for light and shadow and her natural ability for selecting the perfect composition for each picture. "Knows what's true," he said. "Knows how to keep the crap out of her pictures."

Mary finished loading her cameras and lined us up against the wall, as though we were going to be executed. She put Hemingway in the middle, Peter on his left, and me on his right. She started to walk away, then remembered the two females and hurriedly placed them on the flanks, Jigee next to me, Kathie next to Peter. Hemingway stood there patiently, wearing a red-and-white gingham shirt from Abercrombie and Fitch and a checked cap with a peak. Under the shirt he wore a navy-blue turtleneck sweater. When Mary was out of earshot he said, "Remarkable photographer. And with only twenty-six hundred dollars' worth of equipment."

When Mary was about twenty-five yards away, she turned and started to focus the Leica. After not taking any pictures with that camera, she shouted something that we couldn't hear and turned around and ran back another twenty-five yards. Hemingway said, "She probably wants to get the cathedral and the aqueduct in the picture." Mary stopped and began to focus the Hasselblad. As she looked down into the ground glass, Hemingway muttered out of the side of his mouth, "Watch her right hand, that's the one she snaps the shutter with. Just before she snaps it, I'll say, 'Now, right' or 'Now, left' and we'll all jump in whichever direction I say. That way we have a fighting chance to be in the picture."

After our trip to Pamplona, Peter Viertel wrote the screenplay for *The Old Man and the Sea*. Leland Hayward was the producer, Fred Zinnemann, director, and Floyd Crosby, cameraman.

From the beginning, Hemingway was very much in evidence as general expert on Cuban affairs, deep-water fishing, casting (for swordfish and actors), rum drinks at his local bar, The Florida (he called it the Floridita), and anything else that might expedite or hold up the making of the film. He led his own unit to the windswept shores of Peru to photograph real sharks and swordfish. He exposed thousands of feet of film, little of it usable, and after several weeks he brought his unit back to Havana. While he was away, Zinnemann shot what he could with the first unit. The Warner Bros. special-effects department in Burbank had manufactured a mechanical swordfish and shipped it to Cuba. When Hemingway saw it, he was heard to mutter, "No movie with rubber fish makes money."

Floyd Crosby said that they had been incredibly unlucky with the weather, that he had been all over the world, photographing everything from Murnau's *Tabu* to Pare Lorenz's *The River* and Zinnemann's *High Noon,* and that he had never experienced such bad luck. He said that Hemingway thrived on the foul weather but Zinnemann was miserable.

The situation finally got so bad that the shooting stopped. Tracy retired to his villa, ill, Zinnemann retired to his villa, frustrated, and Hemingway invited the crew to the Florida bar for frozen daiquiris.

Shortly after this, Fred Zinnemann did the only thing a responsible film director could have done under the circumstances: he notified Leland Hayward and Warner Bros., the financing company, that he was closing down the picture.

At that time, a million and a half dollars had been spent and Warner Bros. had approximately two hundred usable feet of film (two and a half minutes).

The combatants licked their wounds and prepared to go home. Hemingway was already home, so he put to sea in his fishing boat. When he came back, the movie company had disappeared and the weather was clear for the first time in six weeks.

Warner Bros. later revived the picture with a new director, John Sturges, a new cameraman, James Wong Howe, and a new production approach. All the sea shots were made by a second unit, and Spencer Tracy played his scenes on a soundstage in front of a process screen, a device that projects scenes on a large screen that the actors perform in front of.

The picture was released and well received by some critics, but it failed commercially. With all the troubles, the final cost had risen astronomically and it was practically impossible for the picture to make a profit. Most of the critics praised Tracy, Hemingway, and Viertel.

As far as I know, Hemingway never saw the picture, and I

was told by people who knew him that he declined to comment when the subject came up. He went back to working on a novel and wrote in "A Situation Report" in *Look* magazine:

> The company of jerks is neither stimulating nor rewarding, so for a long time you have tried to avoid it. There are many ways to do this and you learn most of them. But jerks and twerps, the creeps and the squares and the drips flourish and seem, with the new antibiotics, to have attained a sort of creeping immortality, while people that you care about die publicly or anonymously each month. The interruption of the picture is over. There will never be any more picture work ever.

12

Bad Cop/Good Cop

The police work in mysterious ways. One is to assign two detectives to the same case, a bad cop and a good cop. The bad cop grabs the suspect, yells at him at the top of his voice, knees him in the groin, belts him in the mouth, and drags him into the station for questioning by the good cop.

The good cop apologizes for his partner's behavior, gently massages the suspect's groin, puts some of his teeth back in his mouth, and says, "He didn't mean it. He's really a nice guy."

Motion-picture producers sometimes work the same way. Take the case of *Fire Down Below*, the picture I directed in Tobago for Columbia Pictures with Rita Hayworth, Robert Mitchum, and Jack Lemmon at about the time *The Old Man and the Sea* was being shot in Cuba. Our story was by Max Catto, the script by Irwin Shaw. The two producers had been told by Harry Cohn, the Columbia boss in Hollywood, that they could use one of Columbia's one-picture-a-year contractual commitments with me and the same kind of commitments they had with Jack Lemmon and Rita Hayworth — if they could find her. Rita had recently divorced her fourth husband, Dick Haymes, and was hiding somewhere in Europe with her two daughters, one from her marriage to Orson Welles and one from her marriage to Prince Aly Khan. One of my first assignments as director was to find her.

The information center for Americans abroad at that time was Art Buchwald, a close friend of mine, whose column ran in the Paris *Herald Tribune*. He knew everything. I called Art and asked him if he knew where Rita was, and he said, "I'll call you back tonight."

I was staying at the Hotel Lancaster on the rue de Berri in Paris, and I hung around the lobby waiting for Art's call. At 6:00, one of the producers (the less charming one) called and said, "Did you find Hayworth?" I told him that I was working on it.

"Well, ya better find her quick or the picture's off," he said.

"I've got a good lead," I told him.

He said, "Find her!" and hung up.

At 9:00 Art called and said, "She's in suite eight ten at the George V Annex. Give Michel, the concierge, a hundred francs and he'll let you go up without being announced. He's alerted."

I arrived at suite 810 and knocked on the door. There were some padded footsteps, then the door opened and there was Rita Hayworth. She was wearing a simple black dress and no makeup, and she was barefooted. She was also beautiful.

"Yes?" she said.

I introduced myself and asked her if I could talk to her a few minutes about a movie I was making with Robert Mitchum and Jack Lemmon. "Is it going to be shot in Hollywood?" she said.

"No," I said. "We're planning to shoot most of the picture on location in Tobago, with a few interiors at a studio in London. No work in Hollywood."

"Come in, then," she said. She gave me a drink, and I gave her the script with Irwin Shaw's name on it. "I love Irwin's work," she said. "I'll read it tonight." She introduced me to her daughters, Rebecca Welles and Yasmin Khan. They were charming, just as their mother was.

"Does Harry Cohn know you're here?" said Rita.

"He knows about the project and has agreed to let us use your Columbia commitment, but I doubt if he knows I'm here."

"Don't tell him anything," she said. "If it works out, I'll handle it through my agent, Bert Allenberg, and my lawyer, Bartley Crum. Where are you staying?"

"I'm at the Lancaster."

"I'll call you tomorrow morning," she said.

And she did. And she said she liked the script and liked her part, and when did we leave for Tobago? I told her to start packing.

Later in the day Harry Cohn phoned me from Hollywood. "I hear you found Rita," he said.

"Yes, I did," I said.

"How does she look?" said Cohn.

"Beautiful," I said. "She looks beautiful."

"Big deal," said the president of Columbia Pictures. "She always looks beautiful," and he hung up without saying goodbye.

As Rita and I flew to London together, she said, "What are the producers like?"

"They're OK," I said. "Hardworking, hustling. One of them is a very nice guy and the other is a bit on the crude side. He makes a lot of noise, gets everyone riled up, then the nice guy moves in and calms things down."

"And what does the crude one do then?"

"Oh, he usually lies low for a while, then remembers he's a coproducer and starts kicking and screaming again."

"That's what I've been doing. That's what I was doing in Paris."

"Kicking and screaming?"

"No, lying low, hiding. I'm sick and tired of people asking questions about my life with Orson, my life with Aly, my fights with Harry Cohn. I just want to get away. That's why I look forward to doing this picture. It will give me time to think out my life, to get organized." She looked out of the window as the plane started to land and said, "Which producer goes to Tobago with us? Or do they both go?"

"No, we get the quiet one. The kicker and screamer has to stay in London and watch the store."

"Will Harry Cohn have a spy on the set?"

"No," I said. "Why?"

"If he doesn't, it will be the first Columbia Picture I've done without one. Are you sure?"

"No, but if one shows up, we'll ignore him."

Rita smiled and said, "I like this project more every day."

Christopher Columbus discovered Tobago in the fifteenth century. It was a perfect background for *Fire Down Below,* a story of three lost souls, played by Hayworth, Mitchum, and Lemmon.

Hayworth, the famous "love goddess" and "sex symbol," turned out to be more like a kid sister to me, an older sister to Lemmon, and a favorite niece to the avuncular Mitchum. We all liked her and soon learned that she usually depended on some older man, to advise and protect her. This probably led her into her bad marriages. Years of being misunderstood or taken for granted by people, of being treated like a workhorse in the studio on the one hand and being fawned over because of her success on the other, had turned a naturally hesitant, private, and shy girl into a very wary woman.

We chartered a freighter, and a speedboat to carry film, messages, lunches, mail, visitors, et cetera, back and forth between the freighter and the small town of Scarborough. The "good producer" didn't have much to do, so I gave him a small part in the picture. He played a drug smuggler and did it very well. He was also in charge of the courier speedboat from Scarborough. His arrival each morning with the mail was the highlight of our day. For the first few days, Rita didn't get any mail, not even a postcard, and we all felt sorry for her. Then, on the fifth day, she got a bundle bigger than all the rest of the mail put together. We were lounging around the deck reading back issues of *Variety* and the *Hollywood Reporter,* letters from home, whatever.

Suddenly I heard Jack Lemmon scream, "Reeter! What the hell are you doing?" I looked up and saw Rita standing at the rail. She was tearing unopened envelopes in half and throwing them into the sea. Lemmon rushed up to her, grabbed the letters, and said, "Are you crazy? There may be checks in some of these letters!"

"There may be," said Rita, "but there's bound to be more trouble than money."

On the tenth day of shooting, the "good producer" brought Harry Cohn's spy on board the freighter and introduced him as "the Columbia representative." I shook his hand and said, "Welcome aboard," and Rita said, "I wondered when you would show up." Jack Lemmon said, "Nice to meet you," and Mitchum said, "Hello, spy," and that became the fellow's nickname during the twelve weeks he was with us. Not just "spy," but "Hello spy." He was greeted with "Good morning, Hello spy," or "Please pass the butter, Hello spy," and, in the evening, "See you tomorrow, Hello spy." He was a rather bland, bespectacled man with a nervous tic that flared up every time he saw Mitchum. Everyone except the "good producer" ignored him, just as I had promised Rita.

When we came back to London, we were making an important close-up of Rita, and I told Dickey Dickinson, the cameraman, to take special care with it, not to hurry. Rita was playing a woman over the hill but still beautiful, and I wanted her to look her best. Dickey started to work, lighting Rita's stand-in, and I went to my office. After about fifteen minutes, my assistant knocked on my door and came in.

"You better come to the set," he said. "The shit's hit the fan. Rita's in tears, her makeup's streaked, and she's locked herself in her dressing room."

"What the hell happened?" I asked.

"One of the producers came on the set and started yelling at Dickey Dickinson."

"About what?"

"About taking too long to light Rita's stand-in. Dickey told him that you had asked him to take special care with the shot, and the producer said, 'No matter how long you take, Hayworth ain't gonna look any younger.' He turned to me and said, 'Get the director down here and tell him to make the goddamn shot.' I don't think he knew that Rita was on the set and heard everything that was said."

"Then what happened?"

"That's when Rita went to her dressing room, and that's when the other producer came down and tried to get her back on the set, and that's when Rita threw the bottle of acetone at him. She thought he was the screamer."

The picture closed down for two days. Rita refused to appear until the "good producer" guaranteed that the "screamer" would never show up on the set when she was working. She had learned a lot about making movies when she was married to Orson Welles. One of the things she had learned was that it was very expensive to fire a leading player when 90 percent of the picture had been shot.

When we finished the picture, Mitchum, Lemmon, Hayworth, and I had a farewell dinner at Les Ambassadeurs, a fancy Mayfair club. We still liked each other. After dinner, Lemmon took Rita home. Mitchum and I ordered nightcaps and talked about our adventures on the picture. When we got around to Rita, I said, "What's the secret of Rita?"

"The secret of Rita is there's no secret," said Mitchum. "She's just a hell of a nice, simple girl that too many people have been using for too long."

The "screamer" had had his fill of making movies and went into the horse-racing business, where everybody yells all the time and nobody notices it. The "good producer" continued to make movies and became one of the most successful producers in the history of the business. The next time you see a James Bond picture, pay attention to the credits at the beginning. One of them will read "Produced by Albert Broccoli." That was our "good producer."

13

Hemingway
and
How to Write for the Movies
(Part II)

Having been present when Ernest Hemingway first solicited Peter Viertel's help as screenwriter, and having watched the progress of *The Old Man and the Sea* through the *Hollywood Reporter, Variety,* and the Caribbean grapevine, I felt as though I had a proprietary, albeit vicarious, interest in the film. I was (and am) curious about the history of films: how they get made, why they get made, who actually gets them on the screen, and who tries to keep them off. I made it a point to talk to anyone I knew who had been connected with *The Old Man and the Sea.* I had been able to get a firsthand account from most of the participants except Hemingway. My chance to fill in the mosaic came in 1956.

Peter Viertel was in Paris working on a novel. I was in London, having completed shooting *Fire Down Below* and now waiting for the music to be composed. I picked up the phone and Peter's familiar voice said, "Hi, kid. How would you and Kathie like to go back to Spain?"

"I'd like it."

"Great. Here's what we'll do. Ordóñez is fighting in Logroño at the end of September. We'll meet Papa at the Chantaco in St.-Jean-de-Luz on the twenty-first and drive down together."

"We'll be there," I said.

I hung up and my wife said, "What was that about?"

"Peter Viertel says Ernest Hemingway is doing a novel about the Second World War. He's calling it *Foxhole Charlie* and wants to pick my brain about Bob Capa and the Rhine River crossing. Peter says Hemingway particularly asked for me and said if I would come along and help him, I could bring you and we could both call him Papa."

We arrived at the Chantaco on the evening of the twentieth and waited for Peter Viertel and the Hemingways to come in from Paris. After drinks on the patio, Kathie and I sat down to a wonderful candlelit dinner in the dining room. She looked beautiful, we were both young, I was a movie director, the French franc was five to the dollar. The waiter brought a bottle of white wine and poured a little bit into my glass. I sipped it and said to my wife, "That's a Basque wine. It's not French and it's not Spanish and it's clean and it's fresh and it's true." I turned to the waiter and asked to see the bottle. He held it in front of me and it was just like the bottle Hemingway had asked to see three years before. "It's OK," I said. "Give Kathie some of this clean, fresh, true Basque wine from this bottle with no label."

The waiter said, "Comment?" and I said, "Está bueno." He looked at me skeptically, but he poured the wine.

The next morning I looked out of the window and saw Ernest Hemingway. He was sitting by himself at the table under the orange trees. His hair and beard were whiter and his stomach was bigger, but he was wearing the same kind of moccasins he had worn three years before, no socks, and the same kind of checked shirt. He was also wearing dark glasses. "Come on, Lady Brett," I said to my wife. "Ernest Hemingway is waiting for you on the patio."

At breakfast Hemingway said that he and Mary had left Paris the night before and that Peter and Jigee were driving down this morning. Hemingway was enthusiastic about the adventure ahead. He talked to us as though we were experienced aficionados.

"Antonio and Girón are on the bill in Logroño and a new Mexican kid named Joselito Huerta. Pete told me about him, says he saw him in Mexico."

The concierge came in and said that I was wanted on the

phone. As he showed me to the phone in the corner of the main lounge he said, "Parigi."

"Hi, kid, it's Peter."

"Where are you?" I said.

"I'm in Paris, and I'm not going to be able to make it today."

"Why not?"

"I've got some problems here and I can't leave."

"Jesus, I'm sorry," I said. "What kind of problems? Anything I can help you with?"

"No," he said. "Thanks a lot. It's Jigee. She's not well. I'll tell you about it when I see you. Don't tell Papa about Jigee, just tell him I called and said I couldn't make it."

"He's right here, in the dining room. I'll get him."

"No," said Peter. "Don't disturb him. Just tell him I couldn't make it."

When I got back to the table, the two wives had gone to their rooms and Hemingway was having a second cup of coffee. He had taken off his dark glasses, and I could see that his trout-specked eyes looked no older than when I had last seen him. I told him that Peter couldn't come, and Hemingway was obviously disappointed.

"Did he have an accident?" he said.

"No," I said. "He just said to tell you he couldn't make it."

He looked through me for quite a long time, then he looked out of the window at the orange trees. I took a sip of somebody's cold coffee and wished they hadn't put a cigarette butt in it.

Hemingway turned back to me and said, "Tell somebody you're going to be somewhere, only three things can happen: you're there when you said you'd be there, or you don't want to be there, or you're dead." He stood up and said, "Let's go. Logroño's further than Pamplona."

"Maybe you'd rather call the trip off," I said. "Or just drive down with Mary alone."

"No. Said I was going to take you to Logroño. Try to keep all promises, good or bad. Try to be on the spot where I say I'll be even if I have to move other people off it."

As we walked across the dining room, I said, "What time do the bullfights start in Logroño?"

"All corridas in Spain start at five o'clock by law," he said. "The bullfighters and the bulls and the spectators are all there on time because that's when they said they would be there."

The Hemingways led the way south in a new, larger, Lancia. The weather was perfect, and the Austin A-40 kept right up with the Lancia as long as I kept the accelerator right down to the floorboard.

"I can't wait to ask him about the movie," I said.

"What movie?" said my wife.

"*The Old Man and the Sea.* I've talked to practically everyone else connected with the picture and I'm anxious to hear Hemingway's version. That's one of the main reasons I wanted to come on this trip."

"Don't you dare bring that subject up," she said. "You know it must be a sore point with him, and he's got enough troubles without some nosy film buff asking him dumb questions."

"I'm not a film buff," I said. "I'm a paid-up member of the Screen Directors Guild and I'm interested in my work."

"*The Old Man and the Sea* wasn't your work. It was Freddie Zinnemann's and John Sturges's work. Don't you dare bring it up."

She settled back in her end-of-subject position.

I drove on for a while and finally said, "Research."

"I beg your pardon?" said my wife.

"Research. I'm doing research for an article I'm writing. That's why I wish to ask Mr. Hemingway a few questions."

"What's the name of the article?"

" 'How to Write for the Movies.' "

"You just want to probe into the poor man's private affairs and then tell all your pals that Papa told you this and Papa told you that."

"I don't call him Papa."

"No, not to his face, you don't. But I'll bet you he's Papa when his back is turned. I'll bet the gang at Musso and Frank's has been subjected to a lot of Papa time during the past three years."

Musso and Frank's is a very good restaurant on Hollywood Boulevard. Movie people eat there, but they usually talk about movies, not book writers.

"OK," I said. "I promise not to mention *The Old Man and the Sea*. I promise not to mention anything. I'll pretend I'm a deaf mute." We were now passing through a town called St. Domingo de la Calzada. "I'll say I was stricken deaf and dumb in St. Domingo de la Calzada and won't recover until I'm back in Musso and Frank's."

"How will you say it if you're deaf and dumb?" asked my logical helpmate.

"You can say it for me. You can tell Ernest Hemingway that you have forbidden me to talk about a certain subject. If he says, 'What subject?,' you can tell him it's none of his goddamn business."

"So you promise?"

"Yes," I said. "I promise."

Hemingway sat in the front row between the two ladies and I sat right behind them. Hemingway was his usual kind, instructive self to Kathie, explaining everything that happened, but not talking down to her. Ordóñez and Curro Girón were good, but Joselito Huerta, fighting the first bull, was the star of the day. He cut two ears, the tail, and a foot, and the crowd gave him a tremendous ovation. He had dedicated the bull to Hemingway, and he stopped in front of us and held up the two ears and the dung-covered tail and the bloody foot. Hemingway stood up, the crowd went wild, Kathie cried. As the mules dragged the dead bull on a triumphant tour of the ring, Hemingway said, "Some of the best muleta work I've ever seen, *faena cumbre*. Peter was right about the Mexican."

Curro Girón was next. Hemingway told Kathie that he was good, but that he looked even better than he was because he had drawn a great bull. At one point when Girón was working with the muleta, he made the bull turn so sharply that the bull stood there, stunned, staring glazedly at his tormentor. Girón turned his back on the bull and walked arrogantly away. This was the first time Kathie had seen this theatrical trick. She clutched Hemingway's arm and said, "Ohmygod! The bull will kill him!"

Hemingway said nothing. Girón continued his ballet dancer's prance, not looking back. The crowd roared; the bull gasped for breath and so did Kathie.

"What's wrong?" she cried. "Why doesn't he charge?"

"Testicles," said Hemingway.

"What about them?" said my wife.

"When a bullfighter performs a *Dublando con el* the way Girón just did, the testicles swing around and crack against each other so that the testicle owner is in a state of shock and immobilized for fifteen or twenty seconds."

"The poor man," said my wife.

"No, he's all right," said Hemingway. "It's the bull's testicles, the *criadillas*, that swing around. That's why he can't charge the bullfighter."

Ordóñez's bull was troublesome. When Ordóñez tried to kill him, his sword hit a bone in the bull's neck and his hand slipped along the sword. Blood flowed, both human blood and bull blood, and the crowd gasped. Hemingway stood up, concerned, and Kathie said, "What happened?"

"*Pinchazo,*" said Hemingway. "*Pinchar en el duro.* It means to go in a little way and hit bone."

"But his hand's bleeding," said Kathie. "What's he going to do?"

What he did was have a member of his *cuadrilla* wrap a handkerchief around the flesh wound, and then he went out and killed the bull superbly. The crowd cheered and waved handkerchiefs to request that the president of the corrida concede the ear of the bull as a token of honor to the matador. When this happens, if the president agrees and believes the demands to be justified, he will wave his own handkerchief, after which a banderillero may cut the ear and present it to the matador. Hemingway explained that originally the cutting of the ear signified that the bull became the property of the matador to dispose of as beef to his own advantage. This significance has long been obsolete, so the bloody piece of black gristle the banderillero handed Ordóñez was the only tangible evidence he had of his triumph. The T-bones, chump chops, and sirloins were unceremoniously dragged out of the ring.

When the corrida was finished and each matador had acquitted himself reasonably well, Hemingway went to the dispensary to see Ordóñez. Kathie and Mary and I headed back to the hotel. It was September and still warm, so we sat down at a table in the patio and I ordered a bottle of Rioja wine.

"Too bad about Ordóñez's hand," I said. "If it hadn't been for that one mistake, I think he would have been the best of the three."

Even as I said it I thought I shouldn't have, and when Kathie kicked me I was sure.

"It wasn't a mistake," said Mary protectively. "It was an accident that could happen to anybody."

The wine arrived and the waiter filled our glasses. "Yes," I said, "I guess Ordóñez was just unlucky."

"Ordóñez is not unlucky," said Mary, and she left the table.

I swallowed my wine, refilled my glass, and said, "What's wrong with her?"

"Nothing's wrong with her," Kathie said. "It's you. You just insulted Papa's favorite bullfighter. You know how he is about fate and luck and charms and things like that. He's worn that old belt of his for years. I think he took it off a dead German or something. He wouldn't give it up for anything."

"Who's asking him to?" I said. "And what does that have to do with an unlucky bullfighter?"

"Well, it's the beginning of the bullfighting season and everybody's spooky and superstitious about every little thing, and for somebody to blurt out that the best bullfighter in the world is unlucky in the first fight of the season . . . God!"

"Who says he's the best bullfighter in the world?"

"And to say it to Ernest Hemingway's wife . . . Jesus! How insensitive can you get?"

"Not insensitive enough to believe everything anybody tells me," I said. "The poor guy just missed, that's all. He tried to kill the goddamn bull and he missed. If it had been anybody else, Hemingway would have said he was yellow or that he didn't have any balls or something, but because he has decided that Antonio Ordóñez is the greatest bullfighter in the world, I'm not allowed to say he's unlucky."

Hemingway came over and sat down at the table. He was preoccupied, worried, not really with us. He ordered a double Scotch, which surprised me. Up to now he had only been drinking wine. We sat in silence, waiting for the waiter to bring the Scotch. While we were waiting, I knocked off two glasses of red wine, my eighth and ninth. The waiter brought the double Scotch, and Hemingway downed it and ordered another. I drank another glass of red wine too fast and said, "How is Ordóñez's hand?"

Hemingway stared at his empty glass as though he hadn't heard me. The waiter brought the second double Scotch, and after Hemingway downed that one he said to the waiter, "The bottle, please." The waiter brought the bottle and placed it on the table, and nobody moved until I silently held up the empty Rioja bottle with my right hand. With my left hand I made the V-for-victory sign, but in this case I hoped the waiter would interpret it as "Please bring two more bottles of Rioja Spanish red wine to this table where we are having some kind of crisis, to be determined later." It was quite clear from Hemingway's mood that Ordóñez's wound was at least fatal. Poor Hemingway, the only one who knew the facts, turned his empty glass slowly and finally said, "The carpal tunnel," to the glass, not to us. He poured another Scotch and I poured another Rioja. This was the one that made me drunk.

"Luckily the sword didn't touch it," said Hemingway. "It didn't get near the carpal tunnel."

Drunk or sober, I'm pretty good at spotting a conversation stopper, so I downed my wine, got up, and went to the men's room. The men's room in a Spanish town during a fiesta is not a pleasant place to spend much time, but I stayed in the foul-smelling cubicle as long as I could stand it, and when I came back to the table the bottle of Rioja was almost empty and half the bottle of Scotch was gone. Both Hemingway and my wife were staring at their glasses. I sat down and poured myself some Rioja.

"Cheers," I said, hoping that one of them would acknowledge my presence.

My wife said, "Where's the carpal tunnel?"

Without looking up, Hemingway said, "In the wrist. All the tendons that control the hand run through it. The veins, the blood, the sinews too — everything. If you cut that, you're finished."

"Ordóñez is lucky," I said, glancing at Kathie, hoping to get back in with her. "He's lucky the sword didn't hit the old carpal tunnel." She was still staring at her glass, so I ventured, "Antonio Ordóñez sure is a lucky bullfighter."

"No, he's not," said Hemingway. "Not today." He looked at

the palm of his big right hand. "The ball of the thumb is occupied by short muscles called the thenar group. These muscles and the two outer lumbricals are supplied by the median nerve, which runs along here." He pointed to the meaty part of his hand at the base of his thumb. "That's where it got him," he said. "He was bleeding so much I thought he had cut his thumb off." He took another belt of Scotch and I took another belt of Rioja. I was drinking right along with him. I wasn't going to have my wife accusing me later of not drinking along with Ernest Hemingway when he was talking about blood and needed someone to drink along with him.

"How many stitches?" I said.

"You don't count stitches," Hemingway said. "It's unlucky."

"Will they be able to sew the median nerve together?" I said, tap dancing away from the dreaded subject.

"Didn't hit the median nerve. Just got the fleshy part of the hand. Lucky."

I looked at my feet and shut up. The longer this story went on, the luckier the unlucky Ordóñez became.

A lot of people started to yell across the square and we all looked up and saw Ordóñez approaching with a gang of managers, handlers, and hangers on. I thought about what Hemingway had said to the American writer about bullfight followers, but none of them looked like fairies to me. Chairs appeared from somewhere and Ordóñez's immediate gang sat down with us. The rest of the crowd stood around and watched us. Ordóñez had a Band-Aid at the base of his right thumb. He and Hemingway talked in rapid Spanish. Hemingway was usually a slow speaker, but when he spoke Spanish he seemed to shift into a higher gear. I understood enough Spanish to know that they were talking about the *feria* at Zaragoza, which was to start the next day. I didn't hear anybody mention Ordóñez's wound.

After a while Kathie said, "How's your hand?" and Ordóñez said, "*Como?*" Kathie pointed to the Band-Aid and Ordóñez said, "It's nothing. A small cut. Nothing." He smiled and he was charming. Then he said something to Hemingway about meeting him later, and off he went like a queen bee with his swarm of drones and attendants following.

Kathie and I sat there, feeling foolish after all the clinical talk of the cutting off of thumbs and severed median nerves and bleeding to death. Hemingway poured himself another Scotch and poured the last of the Rioja into Kathie's glass. A sad silence again hung over the table. Finally I heard some-one say, "How did the movie go? How did you like shooting *The Old Man and the Sea?*"

I looked around to see who was speaking and discovered that it was me, or I, I don't remember which, and I didn't recognize myself at first because both of us were drunk. Kathie didn't kick me. I never did find out why.

Hemingway downed the last of the Scotch and fixed his still-clear eyes on me. "Weren't you in Pamplona when I gave my speech on how to write for the movies?" he said.

"Yes, I was," I said.

"I should have listened," said Ernest Hemingway.

14

How About That?

Much has been written about Leroy "Satchel" Paige the legendary black baseball pitcher, but, to my knowledge, very little (or nothing) has been written about the same Leroy "Satchel" Paige the film actor.

Tom Lea wrote a wonderful novel and, appropriately, called it *The Wonderful Country*. I bought the film rights and paid Robert Ardrey to write a screenplay. It was the story of Martin Brady (played by Robert Mitchum) and other lost men, going back and forth across the Rio Grande, searching for a country, a place where they could find peace, where they belonged.

The United States Tenth Cavalry, an all-black unit headed by a white major (Colton) and a black sergeant (Tobe Sutton), was important in the story. We cast Gary Merrill as Major Colton but were having trouble finding the right actor to play the sergeant. Bob Mitchum suggested Satchel Paige.

Paige had had a great career with the Kansas City Grays in the black leagues. Then, when Paige was forty-two years old, Bill Veeck brought him to Cleveland, where he helped the Indians win the 1949 World Series. After that, he was with a losing St. Louis Browns team for a couple of years and then went back to the minor leagues and faded out of the national sports pages.

"Where can we find him?" I asked Mitchum.

"Beats the hell out of me," he said. "Why don't you call Bill Veeck? He probably knows."

I called Veeck and he said Paige was now with the Miami

Marlins in the Southern Association, but he didn't think I could get him on the phone because he was in jail on some misdemeanor charge and the judge only let him out on the days he pitched. "The judge is a baseball fan," said Veeck.

I called the judge and explained that this was an opportunity for a new career for Paige, that we would bail him out of his troubles and return him to the team when he completed his part in the picture.

"Well," said the judge, "I think we can work it out. Leroy has a sore arm and has lost his last four games. This could give him some time to rest his arm. I'll let him out if you'll guarantee he doesn't touch a baseball until he comes back to Miami."

"It's a deal," I said.

Paige arrived in Durango, Mexico, a week later. He was accompanied by a beautiful teen-aged black girl whom he introduced as Susan. I knew he had a daughter and I assumed that's who the black beauty was.

Paige soon became a favorite of every member of the cast and crew. He was a tall, dignified man who patiently gave stock answers to the inevitable stock questions about his colorful career. Question: "Hey, Satch, how about giving us your ten maxims for good living?" Answer: (1) "Never look back. Somebody may be catching up on you." (2) "Don't eat fried foods, they jangle your nerves." (3) "The social ramble ain't restful," and so on. Question: "What is your real age?" Answer: " 'Bout the same as yours."

Everyone called him Satch except Mitchum, who called him Leroy. The two stars were attracted to each other from the beginning. Mitchum told Paige about movie acting and Paige told Mitchum about baseball.

MITCHUM: You know you have to ride a horse in the picture, Leroy. You're supposed to be a cavalry sergeant.
PAIGE: Don't worry about it, Robert. You show me how to get on and I'll show you how to get off.
MITCHUM: Tell me about pitching in the majors.
PAIGE: It's about the same as acting in the majors. You just have to keep your eye on the ball.

Paige was perfect as Sgt. Tobe Sutton. He stayed with us for six weeks, and when it was time to send him back to Miami,

Mitchum and I took him to the airport. Susan boarded the small commuter plane, and Mitchum, Paige, and I stood on the Tarmac until the last moment, reluctant to say goodbye. We agreed to keep in touch, and after a while, Mitchum asked Paige a question that had been bothering us since Paige arrived.

"Is Susan your daughter?" he said.

"No," said Paige. "She's my daughter's nurse."

There was a pause and then Mitchum finally said, "But your daughter's not here."

Paige looked at Mitchum and smiled. "How about that?" he said. Then he turned and boarded the plane, still smiling.

The plane taxied to the end of the Tarmac and turned around. As it roared down past us, I think I saw Paige's smiling face in a window. As the wheels left the ground and nestled into the plane's underbelly, Mitchum turned to me and repeated, "How about that?"

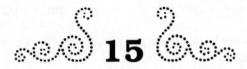
In the French Style

23 EGERTON TERRACE
LONDON SW3 2BU
(01) 589 9072

4 Jan. 1961

Mr. Irwin Shaw
Chalet Mia
Klosters, SWITZERLAND

Dear Irwin;

Thanks for your letter. ИХГ Of course I'd like to
make a movie with you. I thought you'd never ask.

Let's meet in Paris or somewhere.✳ I'll tell you my
ideas, you tell me yours and we'll go with yours.
OK?

All Parrishes send love to all Shaws.

Best,

Bob Parrish

✳ HOW about ON The CESANNA
RUN iN Feb.?

B.

I first met Irwin Shaw in the U.S. Army PX in Paris during the war. He was a warrant officer in the army and I was an enlisted man in the navy. He was trying to buy some Montecristo cigars and I was buying some Colgate toothpaste. The army PX didn't have any Montecristos and Irwin was expressing his disappointment. I didn't want the French clerk to be injured, so I said, "Excuse me, but I think the navy PX over on rue de Presbourg has Montecristos." Irwin said he wasn't in the navy. I said I was and took him over to the navy PX, where he bought two boxes of Montecristo number ones, one box for each of us. I told him I didn't smoke, so he insisted on taking me to lunch at Fouquets on the Champs-Elysées.

We remained close friends for the next forty years. He was the most generous man I ever met in my whole life, even including Sam Spiegel. He was also funny, charming, impossible, gracious, vulnerable, grateful, lovable, irascible, intelligent, impatient, outrageous, noble, prodigious, brave, and honorable. Let's not hear one word said against Irwin Shaw. Not while I'm around.

As I suggested in my letter to Irwin, we met on the Casanna Ski Run in the Swiss Alps. As we skied down to Klosters, we agreed that Irwin would write a screenplay based on two of his short stories. We also agreed to call our company Casanna Productions and our movie *In the French Style*. I was to be the director and Irwin and I would be coproducers. We had a great dinner with our wives, at the Chesa Grischuna Hotel in Klosters, and sealed the deal with a bottle of Dézaley, a Swiss wine.

One of Irwin's short stories on which the script was based was called "A Year to Learn the Language." It was about an American girl in Paris whose father in Chicago agrees to back her art studies for one year. She stays for five years and Paris becomes part of her life. In the script she has to make a big decision: whether to stay in Paris or return to America. A perfect part for Jean Seberg, practically her own story. She was under contract to Columbia Pictures, so I gave the script to Mike Frankovich, the European head of production for Columbia. He liked the script and the rest of the project and suggested that we go to New York with him to set up the deal.

Irwin's agent, Irving "Swifty" Lazar, met us there and we were ushered into the executive conference room of the Columbia offices on Fifth Avenue. Frankovich, four other executives, and two lawyers from Columbia Pictures greeted us. Mike poured some coffee and everyone said how glad he was that Casanna was coming into "the Columbia family." One of the lawyers said, "What's Casanna?" and Lazar said, "That's us." The lawyer said, "Oh."

Irwin and I had told Lazar that it should be a very simple deal because we would take no "up-front money" for (a) the writer, (b) the director, and (c) the producers — us — that we would defer our salaries in return for financial backing and complete control. We would receive nothing unless the picture came into profit. Lazar said we were crazy. We agreed and insisted that that was the deal he was to present.

After the preliminaries about how much everyone liked the script (I knew Mike and Irwin and I had read it, but I wasn't sure about Lazar or anyone else in the room), what the weather was like in California and London, and who was going to win the World Series, Mike said, "What kind of deal do you have in mind, Swifty?"

Lazar jumped to his feet and went into action. "These two guys are crazy," he said, pointing to Irwin and me. "They want to work on spec, and I can't talk 'em out of it." He paused to let his statement sink in. "We're offering you a hell of a script, a fine director, and two top producers who are willing to defer everything and give you a hit picture, and what's Columbia contributing? Money! That's all, just money. You're not picture-makers on this deal, you're investors, like a bank. You lend money."

"How much money?" said the treasurer of Columbia Pictures. "What's the budget?"

Lazar ignored the question. Irwin and I had prepared a very tight budget of $557,000 — much less than Columbia spent on most of their "A" pictures — and Lazar had a copy of it. "You don't seem to understand," said Lazar. "You're not *hiring* these talents, you're going into business with them. You finance, they deliver a picture. You'll be partners."

"What's the budget?" repeated the treasurer.

"My clients are going to have to own a large percentage of the profits, a hell of a large percentage," said Lazar.

"How large?" said the senior vice-president of Columbia.

"Do you know how much Irwin Shaw usually gets to write a screenplay?" yelled Lazar. "Do you know how much Bob Parrish usually gets to direct a picture?"

"Yes, I do," said Mike Frankovich quietly. "We'll pay them their salaries."

At this point, Lazar turned to Irwin and me. "May I have a word with you outside?" he said. We had known Lazar for years, but on this occasion he addressed us as though he were the Secretary General of the United Nations and we were the ambassadors from Sierra Leone and Uruguay. He opened the door and motioned us out of the room. "Excuse us for a moment," he said to the assembled lawyers and executives. He led us to an office down the hall. "I think you fellows should wait in here," he said.

"Why?" said Irwin.

"Because this is gonna get rough," said Lazar. "I'm gonna have to take off the gloves when I go back." He turned and headed for the front lines, closing the door behind him: four feet eight inches of sheer determination.

"What the hell's going on?" said Irwin.

"Lazar is taking off his gloves," I said.

"The deal is so simple. Why is he making it so complicated?"

"Because he's an agent," I answered.

"The guy kept asking him about the budget," said Irwin. "Why didn't Lazar answer him? It's no secret. Frankovich knows what it is. His secretary typed it for us, for Christ's sakes."

"Lazar is embarrassed to represent a picture with such a low budget," I said. "It's a matter of pride with him."

"So what are they doing in there now?"

"Remember that big conference table?" I said. Irwin nodded. "Well, they've got Shaw and Parrish laid out on it and they're cutting us up. Frankovich is saying, 'Here's a leg for you, Swifty,' and Lazar is saying, 'You're too generous, Mike. You take the leg and one of the left arms and add fifty thousand dollars to the budget. Or, better yet, make the budget an even seven hundred fifty thousand and cut off anything you like.' "

Irwin said, "Do you really believe that? Do you think Lazar got us out of the room so he could screw us?"

"What I think is unimportant, and how they cut us up is relatively unimportant, because all we want is to make the picture our way, with no interference. If we get that, we've won."

The phone rang and I answered it. Mike Frankovich's soothing voice said, "Bob, you and Irwin are lucky fellows. You've got the best agent in the business. He murdered us. Come on back in and celebrate."

Before I hung up, Lazar burst in and said, "It's all set. It was tough, but we got the deal we wanted and they raised the budget to three-quarters of a million dollars. They're good people to deal with."

"The budget we made was very tight, but accurate," I said. "What do we need an extra hundred and ninety-three thousand dollars for?"

"Don't worry about it," said Lazar. "We'll find a use for it."

"What about control?" said Irwin.

"About what?" said Lazar.

"Control," said Irwin. "The right to make the kind of picture we want to make with no interference. That's the main reason we're making the goddamn picture."

"No problem," said Lazar. "You have full artistic control until the first preview and a good percentage of the profits. Now, all you have to do is make a good picture and stay within the budget."

Billancourt Studios is on the Seine on the outskirts of Paris, and it is a delightful place to make a movie. There are a bar and restaurant on the premises. If you are a lucky and clever producer, you can arrange to have your sets built on stage A, which has a connecting door to the bar-restaurant. My partner, Irwin Shaw, was both lucky and clever. Shortly after we returned to Paris, he made arrangements for us to shoot our movie on stage A at Billancourt Studios on the Seine.

I went to Barcelona to see Jean Seberg and convince her

to play the lead in *In the French Style*. She was staying in an apartment with her husband, Romain Gary, the writer-diplomat. They had also rented a cottage on the sea nearby. Romain greeted me warmly and said that Jean had broken her foot and was in bed. He took me to the bedroom where Jean was lying on her back with a wire cage over her right foot to protect it from the weight of the blankets. Except for the broken foot, she looked just right for the part Irwin had written. We talked a bit, and Jean suggested that I spend the night at the beach cottage with Romain. She said she would read the script and that we would talk about it the next day.

"How long do you think you will be laid up?" I said. "We're supposed to start shooting in three weeks."

"That won't be a problem," she said. "The cast comes off next week."

A maid brought Jean's dinner on a tray, and Romain and I drove to the cottage. He lit a fire, broiled two giant Mediterranean lobsters, and opened some cold Marques de Riscal white wine.

I had met Romain when he was the French consul in Los Angeles. We talked about the Hollywood movie industry, his work in the diplomatic corps, and his meeting with President Kennedy. I brought up the subject of Irwin's script and whether or not he thought Jean would like the part.

"It sounds fine, but I don't like to get involved in Jean's work," he said. "She makes her own decisions." This was a good sign.

The next day Jean said, "If I don't get this part, I'll never speak to you or Irwin again. I love it."

I returned to Paris and started active preproduction work at Billancourt. Although Lazar had squeezed $750,000 out of Columbia, I was determined to bring the picture in under our original $557,000 budget. Our production manager, Madame Ludmilla Goulian, was a great help. When I told her we wanted to make the picture on the cheap, she promptly canceled the three limousines that Columbia had hired, one each for the two stars and one for the producer-writer-director team. She replaced the three limousines and three chauffeurs with one taxi, owned by one white Russian refugee named Grischa.

"The producer and director usually arrive an hour or two

before shooting," she said. "Grischa will take you and Irwin to Billancourt and go back and get the actors. He'll be at the studio as a standby car until you finish shooting, and then he'll take you all back to Paris. You can take turns riding backwards in the jump seats. After you leave, I'll wind things up at the studio, then Grischa can come back and take me home. After he drops me off, he can work his regular taxi route in Montmartre. In addition to his fees, I've agreed to pay for all of his gasoline. For the whole picture our transportation cost will be less than the cost of one limousine." Madame Goulian's schemes worked perfectly, on the transportation and all other production matters.

On the night before the first day of shooting, Irwin and I had dinner at the Berkeley, one of his favorite restaurants. We were fully cast, fully prepared, and fully happy. We each had two drinks before dinner, drank a fine wine, chosen by Irwin, with our meal, and were now enjoying a cognac.

"Bobby," said my partner, "I'm going to tell you something every director wants to hear."

"I'm a listening director," I said and ordered another cognac for each of us.

"I'm making a firm rule," said Irwin. "I'm not going to interfere on the set. The director's got to be the boss there. In fact, I'm going to Klosters tomorrow for a few days. It will give you a chance to get started and settle down without someone looking over your shoulder. When I come back, I'll be in the office or in the bar. If you want any changes made in the script, we'll make them together after shooting or early in the morning."

The cognacs came. We touched glasses and said, "Good luck to us."

We sipped our drinks, and after a while Irwin said, "What's the first thing you're going to shoot tomorrow?"

"The scene with Jean and the models," I said. "We've got these five beauties coming in for the first setup."

Irwin looked at me through hooded eyes, sipped his cognac, and said, "Well, it's the first day of shooting, and we're co-producers, so I'm going to make an exception to my rule. What time do you start?"

"The girls come in at noon," I said.

"I'll be there," said my partner. And he was.

And throughout the shooting he was always supportive, especially in crisis situations like this. He would come onto the set from time to time and stay until he got bored or until we had some frustrating technical problem. He would then say, "Bobby, you're the director. I don't want to interfere." And he would drift away through the connecting door to the bar or to our office to take care of some of the many details involved in making a motion picture. He later wrote:

> In doing this movie we performed a pleasant duty — we saluted the regiments of American girls who swarm delightfully into Paris every year, to study, to work, to sightsee, to hang around. They are for the most part young, pretty, and adventurous, qualities to please the eye and charm the heart of any American. Or any Frenchman, for that matter. Or any man who has ever leaned against the parapet on the banks of the Seine and brooded over that flowing monument.
>
> But I would not like to give the impression that being a producer is all honey and rose petals. I found myself faced with surprising chores and the necessity of making decisions in fields in which I had to disguise the fact that I had no competence whatsoever. For example — I went through a long, heroic struggle with a hairdresser over the problem of how Miss Seberg's hair was to be combed. Faithfully trying to fulfill what I thought was a co-producer's function, I gave interviews in French for radio and television, shuddering all the time at what my hearty New York accent must have sounded like as it invaded living rooms from Brussels to Monte Carlo. I went to the Film Festival in Venice to pick an actor off the beach, although I had carefully refrained from attending film festivals all my life. I signed orders for toupees and wrote letters of consolation to actors whose performances were left on the cutting room floor. I struggled with musicians, although my entire musical education had been compressed into one year of piano lessons, during which time I just barely mastered one small piece, entitled, The Spinning Song. I called doctors at all hours of the day and night for American actors who

invariably contracted intestinal flu the day before
they were due to appear on the sound stages for the
first time. I re-wrote the script almost entirely as we
went along, something that no other producer
would have been able to persuade me to do. I in-
spected dozens of Great Danes and Russian Wolf-
hounds and hired two of the beasts and later con-
curred in the decision to drop them from the
picture.

The script called for a sequence in a small sail-
boat in a day of absolute windless calm. During the
afternoon before the day on which the scene was to
be shot we heard from the French weather bureau
that high winds and a rolling sea were expected for
the morrow.

A council of war of all the production people was
called and the problem examined from all sides.
Our movie was being made on a modest budget and
losing a day's shooting would have been uncomfort-
ably costly. The problem was finally solved by my
agreeing to report at the dock in Cannes with the
rest of the company at seven o'clock in the morning,
with a pencil in my hand. I had to promise I would
write a scene to match the weather which would
have the same elements and the same emotional
effect as the original one. Luckily, I was not put to
this literary and naval test. I was on the wharf, with
pencil, at seven o'clock, but the sky was sunny, the
sea like glass, and there was not a breath of wind
until we had all safely disembarked, with the scene
safely in the camera.

This all took place on the day that President Kennedy issued his ultimatum to the Russians to get
their missile installations out of Cuba. A large
American aircraft carrier was moored inshore, with
every one of its planes on deck, ready, as far as we
could tell, to take off for Moscow at a moment's
notice. At the same time, in another hemisphere,
Soviet ships were approaching Cuba and the first
encounter with our Navy was expected at any moment. I spent half the day looking at actors and the
other half looking nervously over at the carrier to
see if the planes were taking off. It was about this

time that I told Parrish that I was seriously thinking
of changing the name of our company to Novels
Hereafter Productions.

In closing, let me say that I have never worked
with a group of people who were more loyal, de-
voted, efficient, or agreeable as friends and co-
workers than the people on whom we depended to
help us make our movie in the studio at Billancourt.
However, they present two temptations. The first is
to make another movie with them immediately. The
other is, never to make another movie again, as it is
impossible that we could ever find the same hal-
cyon climate in any studio a second time."

Irwin was right.

It was indeed a happy picture. On the last day we had to
work late to finish under schedule and under budget. When I
finally said, "Cut, print," on the last shot, at 11:30 P.M., Irwin
came in from the bar and invited the cast for dinner at an
elegant restaurant nearby.

"It's too late, Irwin," I said. "The waiters will be going
home and the chef'll be drunk. Let's all go to the bistro on the
corner."

"Nonsense," said my partner. "We're going to the restaurant. Faces will light up."

He insisted, so we all went over to the restaurant. The front
door was locked. We looked in through the window and saw
the maitre d', the chef, and five waiters having a meal at two of
the back tables. Irwin knocked on the door. The maitre d'
came to the door with a napkin tucked under his collar. He
opened the door and saw Irwin, and sure enough, his face lit
up. He beamed, held out both hands, and said, "Monsieur
Shaw! Come in!"

The chef's and the five waiters' faces lit up too when Irwin
gave them money. They served a perfect meal. Someone produced an accordion, someone else produced a harmonica, and
Irwin produced the best end-of-the-picture party I've ever
been to. We sang and danced and swore that we would never
work on another picture with anyone except each other.

I danced with Jean Seberg. "Do you want to know a secret?" she said.

"I don't think so," I said.

"Remember the broken foot I had when you came to Barcelona?"

"Of course."

"Well, my foot wasn't broken," she said. I decided it would be dumb to say anything, especially when I didn't have anything to say. "I was nine months pregnant," she said. I kept dancing, but I slowed down a bit. I still didn't say anything. "Romain and I rigged the wire cage over my foot to hide the pregnancy until after I had read the script. If I liked the script, we would go on with the broken-foot story. If I didn't like it, I was going to tell you everything."

I finally decided I had to say something. "Did you have the baby?"

"Yes," she said, "five days before we started to shoot. A boy."

"And you kept it a secret through the whole picture?"

"It's still a secret. Only you and I and Romain know."

"Why did you do it?"

"Because I loved Irwin's script," she said.

In the French Style was well received commercially and critically. Irwin and I were paid our deferments plus modest profits.

The Kinematograph Weekly critic wrote, "This is a model case of film making. The partnership of Robert Parrish and Irwin Shaw has made a fine job of production, direction and writing. . . . *In the French Style* deserves to be everyone's style."

16

Credits and Debits

After the fun and satisfaction of making *In the French Style*, the European pictures that I was involved in became progressively less interesting.

Casino Royale was a bastardized, episodic parody of Ian Fleming's James Bond films in which each episode had a different James Bond and a different director. For example, David Niven played Bond in John Huston's episode, and Peter Sellers played Bond in my episode, with Orson Welles as Bond's archenemy, Smersh.

After a few days of shooting, I discovered that Welles was at his best in the mornings. After lunch he would become sleepy or tired or lazy or bored. When Sellers discovered this about Orson, he had his agent call Charlie Feldman, the producer, and tell him that Sellers would have to do all of his scenes with Orson late in the afternoon or he, Sellers, would probably forget his lines. "His memory's not very good in the morning," said the agent.

Feldman, an ex-agent himself, said, "We're shooting an important scene with Sellers and Welles tomorrow. You tell your client to get his ass on the set, in costume and makeup, at nine A.M. Tell him I've got a lousy memory too, and if he's not there, I'll probably forget to mail you his check at the end of the week."

Sellers's agent called back fifteen minutes later and said that his client would be there as per contract, that it was just a misunderstanding.

Feldman hung up. "The misunderstanding," he said to me, "is that Orson is a pro and is acting Sellers off the screen, and Sellers hates his guts for it."

The next morning, at 8:45, Welles strode onto the set with his beard trimmed, his face made up, and his 340-pound majestic figure impeccably outfitted in a white dinner jacket. He greeted me enthusiastically and took a position beside the camera.

"Good morning to all!" he bellowed to the crew. They waved and applauded, and Welles bowed deeply in three directions. He was handed a cup of coffee and started to tell wonderful anecdotes about his theater and film experiences, his opinions about the political situations throughout the world, his preference for London cabs (and drivers) over New York cabs (and drivers), his favorite restaurants (and their menu specialties) in the major cities of the world, and so on.

At exactly 9:02 A.M. my assistant took me aside and said that Peter Sellers had called and asked if Orson was on the set.

"Where did he call from?" I asked.

"Somewhere along the A-Three," he said. "He has a phone in his limousine. It's part of his contract."

"What did you tell him?"

"I told him Welles was here and was telling the crew about a great seafood restaurant in Barcelona."

"And what did Peter say?"

"He said, 'Bully for him,' and then he hung up."

"He didn't happen to say where he was on the A-Three, did he?"

"No, he just hung up."

At 10:15 A.M. Orson was still standing by the camera. He had a fresh cup of hot coffee and was now telling the crew about his experiences in Brazil. My assistant advised me that Sellers had called several times and was now five miles from Shepperton Studio and closing in fast.

At 11:06 A.M. Sellers crept in the back door of our stage. He was wearing a pair of blue jeans, a sweatshirt, and dirty sneakers. He was unshaven. James Bond he wasn't.

Welles spotted him and said in a loud, authoritative voice, "Welcome, Mr. Sellers! How good of you to join us!" He turned to the chief electrician and said, "Eddie, please put the spotlight on Mr. Sellers!" The spotlight was focused on Peter and Orson started to applaud. "Let's have a big hand for Mr. Sellers!" he said. The whole company applauded enthusiastically.

Peter stood, startled, in the bright light for a few seconds. Then he turned and disappeared through the back door. He wasn't seen again for two days. His agent advised Feldman that Sellers would come back only if he didn't have to speak to Welles, on or off the screen, for the rest of the shooting. Feldman agreed and Orson agreed.

This created a unique directing job for me — the first picture I ever worked on where the two leading players wouldn't speak to each other, a situation that kept me on my toes and my hand in the aspirin bottle.

The second picture I directed in which the two leading stars were not speaking to each other was called *The Bobo*. Peter Sellers was again the leading man and his wife, Britt Ekland, was the leading lady. The exteriors were shot in Barcelona and the interiors at Cinecitta Studio in Rome.

After three weeks' shooting in Rome, Peter called me aside and whispered, "I'm not coming back after lunch if that bitch is on the set."

"Tell me which one and I'll take care of it," I cringed. He had already had the script girl fired. I figured it was the makeup girl's turn.

"The one over my left shoulder, in the white dress. Don't look now," he said, and slinked away to charm the cast and crew.

The girl in the white dress was his wife and co-star, Britt. It was 11:15 A.M., but I told my assistant to call lunch while I scurried off to my office and called the producer in London. That's where he produced from. He was much too clever to appear where the action was. I told him the expensive story: it would cost Warner Bros. about $71,428.57 per day if Sellers actually refused to show up.

"Don't worry about it," said my sympathetic producer. "I'll fly down tomorrow." I went to the Cinecitta commissary for lunch. The first thing I spotted was Peter and Britt, lunching together, cozy-cozy. As I passed their table, they raised their glasses to me.

They weren't divorced until just after we finished shooting.

Then there was *Up From the Beach*, a post–D Day picture that Darryl Zanuck produced, primarily because he had thousands of feet of film left over from his hit war picture *The Longest Day* and, even more primarily, because we had a girl in *Up From the Beach* that Zanuck liked to visit on our Normandy locations. He confided to me that he was grooming her for stardom.

The Marseilles Contract was shot in Nice, Paris, and Marseilles. It was a pleasure working with James Mason, Michael Caine, and Anthony Quinn. We all tried, but sometimes you win and sometimes you lose.

One of our studio representatives, Raymond, was an interesting character. His strategy was clear: to hang on, by any expedient, any compromise, any dodge, any lie, any means at all, until something turned up. If he could live a day, he could live two; if two, three; if three . . .

He was very involved in some aspects of the production, less so in others. For example, he didn't seem to care much about the script, the photography, or the performances, but he paid strict attention to small details like insisting that James Mason's character in the picture have the same initials as his and that Mason be impeccably dressed, with monogrammed shirts from Sulka and a nine-piece set of monogrammed luggage from Louis Vuitton. Then, when the picture was finished, our Raymond inherited these bits of wardrobe and props, with his initials, as his perks.

On a Sunday, after we had been shooting for two weeks, he burst into my room at the Tremoille Hotel in Paris. "I just talked to Bill in London," he said. "He confirmed the rumor: there's a toilet-paper shortage in the U.K." Bill was the studio representative in London.

"Did he say anything about the rushes?" I asked cautiously.

Raymond looked at me as though I had asked him about the

CREDITS AND DEBITS   137

presidential campaign of Millard Fillmore. "What rushes?" he said angrily.

I realized I was cutting across his toilet-paper train of thought, and it always upset him to have the subject changed to something that he was not interested in. "The rushes on this two-million-dollar movie that I am directing and Bill's studio is cofinancing," I said. "It's called *The Marseilles Contract.*"

He rolled his sad eyes around a few times and hunched his shoulders farther forward the way he did whenever the conversation was not about him personally. "Yeah," he said. "They're OK, but he also said his wife went to six supermarkets, all the way from Shepherd's Bush to Fulham, and she could get only four rolls and one of them was that slick, waxy kind that they have in tube stations, the kind that your finger breaks through unless you fold three or four squares together."

"I'm sorry about Bill's wife's finger," I said. "Did he say anything else about the rushes? Did he like the scene in the park with Michael Caine and Tony Quinn? It's one of the most important scenes in the picture, you know, and we haven't had a lab report. I'd hate like hell to have to shoot it over."

The words *shoot it over* finally brought him around to our film. Retakes could cost money, and money was high on Raymond's priority list, higher even than a toilet-paper shortage in England, especially when we were in Paris and not due to return to London for four weeks.

"Shoot it over!" he screamed. "What in the hell are you talking about? Bill said the stuff is OK. In fact, he said it's great, the best so far."

"Yes, but has he actually seen the film?"

"Of course he has. Would he tell me it was great if he hadn't seen it?"

"I don't know," I said. "Maybe he's got other things on his mind. Maybe he's wondering why his wife hangs around the toilets in tube stations."

"Who says she hangs around tube stations?"

"You did. You just told me that's where she gets her waxy toilet paper."

"I didn't say that. You're misinterpreting again. I simply

quoted the European head of our studio on the toilet-paper situation in London. I didn't say anything about his wife hanging around tube stations. Christ, you know Mildred. Why the hell would she hang around a tube station?"

"Who knows? Maybe she's a good mother and figures she can pick up a few extra sheets of waxy toilet paper for the house. They have these fancy ladies' rooms on the Victoria Line. At the new Tate Gallery station, they even have Kleenex and a makeup table. Maybe she goes in there and cops a handful of Kleenex. It's even softer than regular toilet paper. How the hell do *I* know why Mildred hangs around tube stations? In any event, I'm bored with the conversation. We wouldn't even have known about this dumb subject if Bill hadn't told you about it. I don't believe there *is* a toilet-paper crisis."

As soon as I said it, I realized I'd gone too far. Raymond turned a purplish grey. The tempo of his asthmatic breathing increased, and he picked up the phone and put in a call for Bill in London. The operator said she would call back. While we were waiting for the connection, I poured myself a drink and offered him one. He refused. Finally the phone rang and he dived for it.

"Hello, Bill," he said. "I'm sitting here with Bob Parrish. I'll put him on."

As I took the phone, I remembered the issue: the toilet-paper shortage in England.

"Hi, Bill," I said. "I'm sorry about Mildred's finger."

"What's wrong with her finger?" he said.

"Raymond said she had some trouble in the ladies' room in the Tate Gallery tube station."

"What the hell are you talking about? Mildred's fine, and she never travels by tube. She uses the company limousine. I'm the one who has to go by tube."

"Well, maybe I got it wrong. It was probably your finger that broke through the toilet paper. Anyway, Raymond's really worried. He says you can't buy toilet paper in London. He says . . ."

"Did you guys call me to talk about toilet paper? You're supposed to be shooting a two-million-dollar picture in which our studio is investing half. I hate to change the subject, but how's it going?"

"Not bad," I said. "We finished the big scene with Caine and Quinn, and Raymond tells me you liked the rushes."

"What rushes? I won't see that stuff until tomorrow."

"Then you haven't actually seen the park scene yet?"

"Of course not. I told Raymond that." he paused. "Have you guys been drinking?"

"No," I said. "Sorry to have bothered you. Call me after you've seen the rushes." I hung up. "He hasn't seen a god-damn foot of the scene," I said to Raymond.

He was fifteen feet across the room, picking his nose, but I could feel the defensive adrenaline start to flow. "So what?" he said.

"So you lied to me again, that's what. You told me Bill thought the rushes were great, and the sonofabitch hasn't even seen them. That's a lie, Raymond, and a harmful lie. A lot of us are breaking our asses trying to make a movie, and you keep crossing us up with your chickenshit lies. Now what did you gain by telling me that Bill had seen the rushes? Did it help you? Did it make money for you? Did it keep you out of trouble? Why did you do it? Why do you always lie when it's easier to tell the truth? I'm really curious."

He walked over to the window and looked out at the Paris rooftops. Silence hung over the room for a long time. Finally he said, "Everything would have been OK if you hadn't been so goddamned skeptical. If you hadn't doubted my word about the toilet-paper shortage, I would never have called Bill and you would have thought the rushes were great." You could feel him start to believe in himself, to regain his confidence, planning his attack. "Now, because of your lack of trust, you don't know if the rushes are good or bad." He lit a cigarette and started to pace around the room like a caged tiger. He was really rolling now, starting to yell. "I hope you're satisfied," he said. "I try to tip you off to a situation so that you can stock up on a scarce item and protect yourself and your family, and you call me a liar." He stopped pacing and focused his burning, wounded eyes on me. "What kind of relationship is that, for Christ's sakes? Whatever happened to mutual trust?"

"I trust you on the toilet paper," I said, "and I appreciate what you're trying to do for Kathie and me and the kids in that area." His eyes sank deeper, darker, waiting for me to say something that would give him an exit line. "It's just the whole movie," I said, "and everything else *except* the toilet paper that you lie and cheat on."

"You don't trust anybody!" he screamed. He stormed out of the room and down to his suite at the end of the hall.

A few minutes later my phone rang and Raymond said, "Can I ride to the studio with you tomorrow?"

I said, "Sure. Where's your driver?"

"I'm sending him around Paris to the supermarkets to buy toilet paper. I'm not going to be caught short when we get back to London. You're going to be sorry you didn't listen to me. There'll be no shortage in *my* house."

"I'm not worried, Raymond," I said. "I'm sure you'll share. After all, what are friends for?"

III

DON'T LOOK BACK

17

Birth of a Salesman

We lived in a beautiful five-story Queen Anne house on Egerton Terrace, London SW3. It was one block off the Brompton Road, four blocks from Harrods, and one mile from my seventh-floor office at Marble Arch, where Park Lane met Oxford Street and I met my beautiful secretary named Caroline each morning at 9:00.

After she brought me a cup of coffee and closed the door between our offices, I turned my chair around and stared down at Speakers' Corner in Hyde Park. A movie director without a movie to direct is like a pilot without a plane to fly. After a while, Caroline came in and said, "Do you have anything for me to do?" She had already typed my address book three times, answered all my correspondence, paid my bills, and done everything else that good secretaries are supposed to do. Now she was bored.

I was too. The scripts that were offered to me were second rate and became second-rater as time went by. I tried to get some projects started on my own, but they all fell through. The market for American directors in Europe had softened.

"Do you mind if I ask you a question?" said Caroline.

"Be my guest," I said.

"What do you do in here all day?" she said.

I thought for a minute and then said, "I'm writing a book."

"Oh," said Caroline. "I thought you were just in here staring out of the window."

"That's what writers do," I said.

"Who's typing it?"

"It's not ready to type," I said. "When it is, you'll be the first to know."

"What's the book about?"

"It's bad luck for writers to talk about their work."

She went back to her office.

The next morning, as I walked across Hyde Park, I thought about Caroline, lurking in the outer office. As I passed her desk, I said, "Good morning," and when she brought my coffee in, I said, "Get your pad. I want you to take some dictation." She came back with her pad and pencil and settled down in front of my desk. I got up and stode around the room.

"Where I grew up," I said, "there were two movie theaters: the Lyric and the Royal. The Lyric had a piano over on the left side, down front, near the screen. The Royal had an organ that came up from the pit, complete with organist, as the lights went down in the theater."

"You're going too fast," said Caroline. "Slow down. Is this a script?"

"It's not a script," I said. "It's the book I told you I was writing."

"What's it called?" said Caroline.

"*Growing Up in Hollywood*," I said.

She smiled and said, "Jolly good. Go on."

"That's all I've got, so far," I said. "Type that and we'll go from there."

And we did.

"This is your first book," said my editor on the transatlantic phone. "You can't expect anyone to buy your book if they've never heard of it, can you?"

"No," I said, "I guess not." Silence. "Hello, Tony?"

"Yes, I'm here," said Tony Godwin. "I wish I could make you see how important it is for you to come to America and plug your book, even if it's only for a short time. I can organize the important interviews in New York so that you will spend five days here at the beginning of the tour and three days at the end. In between, we'll shoot you out to the Coast, and on your return trip you can stop in Chicago. You'll be back home in London in less than a month. So there you are."

"Where?"

"In the bookselling business," said Tony. "In today's market, you can't sell books unless you talk about 'em. It's all word of mouth. That's why we have talk shows — Johnny Carson, Irv Kupcinet, Merv Griffin, all that. People don't read books, they *talk* about them. And nobody's going to talk about your book unless you talk about it first."

"I wrote the book. Do I really have to talk about it too?"

"Only in New York, L.A., and Chicago."

"What about Washington?"

"What about it?"

"It's the capital of the United States. Shouldn't I stop there?"

"You're not running for president," he said. "You're selling books. Washington is not a book town."

"Are you sure?" I asked. "I thought all those lawyers and senators and Lockheed representatives might want to read something besides the *Congressional Record*."

"They do. They read *Penthouse* and *Playboy* and the *National Enquirer*. Forget Washington." Pause. "Look, it's a question of money. I don't know exactly how much I'm going to be able to squeeze out of the advertising budget for this tour. I may as well tell you that I'm meeting with a lot of resistance from upstairs. It's very tight already."

"What's upstairs?"

"The executive offices," said Tony. "The money."

"How much have they got up there?"

"They don't actually keep it in cash. It's in a bank somewhere or in tax-free bonds. The guys upstairs make the decisions about how much of it to allot to each book."

"How much are they going to allot to us?"

"Like I told you, we can manage New York, L.A., and Chicago," he said. "Any side trips are on you." Silence again, from London this time. I was adding up what it would cost to stop over in Washington: air fare (maybe I could sneak that in on the transcontinental flight), taxi to N.Y. airport, taxi from Washington airport, hotel for one night, extra meals, taxi back to Washington airport, tips, et cetera, et cetera. I was in the middle of the second et cetera when my editor said, "Hello, operator, I think we've been cut off."

"No, I'm here, Tony," I said. "I was just doing some calculations."

"About what?"

"About how much I can allot to this book. You know, like the guys upstairs."

"And what did you decide?"

"Who pays for my air fare from London?"

"Buy your ticket there," said Tony, "and I'll get you a reimbursement."

"OK."

"Economy."

"Naturally."

"The publication date is May fifth, so if you could be in New York on the first, we'll clear the decks and go to work. When we finish here, you can cover L.A. and Chicago."

"I'd still like to stop over in Washington and see Art Buchwald, even if I don't sell him any books."

"You know Art Buchwald?"

"Sure, he's a good friend of mine."

"Will he mention your book in his column?"

"No."

"Then why stop in Washington?"

"Because he's a friend of mine."

"OK, go ahead. Stop there if you feel you must, but I'm telling you, it's not an important city, bookselling-wise. In any event, you'll go right from there to L.A."

When I arrived in Washington, Art Buchwald, the famous columnist, invited Edward Bennett Williams, the famous lawyer, and an unknown author, me, to lunch at Sans Souci. Art ordered an avocado, a steak, and a green salad. I ordered shad roe, which, for some reason, you can't get in London, and Edward Bennett Williams ordered two raw carrots and a cup of tea, with lemon. We talked about politics and Edward Bennett Williams's diet and the coming baseball season and how it is unwise to have an affair with a secretary, especially if she's your own secretary and especially in Washington. Somebody remembered that Ernest Hemingway had said, "Never with secretaries," and Williams remembered that, after he got out of law school, his first boss had passed along the same advice, but with saltier language. The crusty old gentleman had summoned young Williams into his office and said, "We have two rules here: wear a tie, and don't dip your pen in the company ink."

Williams wore a tie and I guess he kept his pen dry, because he rose to be the senior partner in the firm, bought the Washington Redskins, was chosen treasurer of the Democratic Party, and became one of the most distinguished lawyers in America.

"How long are you going to be in Washington?" he asked.

"Just a couple of days," I answered.

"Bob's written a book," Art said. "He's over here promoting it."

Williams asked what it was about, and I told him it was about growing up in Hollywood and that's what it was called. Williams said he would buy a copy. When Art told him it would cost ten dollars, Williams said, "It had better be good, then."

Art said he was taking me to some bookstores to introduce me to the managers, and then he would keep talking to the managers so I could sneak around and put copies of my book in more prominent display positions, on top of David Niven's book and close to *The Final Days* and Gore Vidal's *1876*. Williams said he thought that was a pretty good idea. Art paid the bill and we headed for the door, but it took us seventeen minutes to get out of the restaurant because Art kept being stopped by senators, ambassadors, movie stars, cabinet ministers, and people like that.

While Art was busy being a celebrity, Williams and I hung around in the background like two of Shirley Temple's fathers. "Is this your first book?" he said.

"Yes," I said. That didn't seem like enough of an answer, so I added, "Yup, this is the first one." Williams didn't say anything, and Art was still on his charm circuit, so I felt obliged to fill in the conversational gap. I considered "There's got to be a first time for everyone," abandoned that, and almost said "Once bitten, twice shy." I knew a cliché was called for, but I just couldn't find the right one. "Here today, gone tomorrow" was dead wrong, as was "Any port in a storm," "Every cloud has a silver lining," and "It never rains but what it pours." I decided to skip the weather and was on the verge of saying "You can't win 'em all" when Art said, "Let's go."

Williams said that being a writer must be the most satisfying profession of all, that writers meet interesting people, work only when they feel like it, and are always being fawned over, asked for autographs, and invited out to fancy dinners. Art said something about the company ink being your own ink when you're a writer, and Williams said, "That's what I mean." I didn't see the connection, and while I was trying to work it out, Williams thanked Art for the two carrots and the tea with lemon and wished me good luck with the book. "I hope you hit the best-seller list," he said.

"Not much danger of that," I said.

"Well, you can't win 'em all," said the owner of the Washington Redskins.

The manager of the first bookstore greeted Art warmly and said he was always glad to meet new writers. He then went into approximately the same speech we had just heard from Edward Bennett Williams, about how being a writer must be the best job in the world. When he got to the part about all the interesting people that writers meet, Art took out a cigar and started to light it. As the bookseller droned on, Art took off his glasses and wiped them with his handkerchief, and when he put them back on I thought he winked at me. It may have been only a blink, but I took it as a signal, and when Art asked the bookseller what he thought of Jimmy Carter's chances, I slithered away, looking for my book.

When your first book is published, you come to know the jacket pretty well, especially the spine, the edge. The fact is, you can usually spot it from about fifty yards. Your eyes scurry past all the best-sellers, the gardening books, the how-to books, the latest Harold Robbins, the newest Irving Wallace, Lillian Hellman's *Scoundrel Time*, the yoga, the Dianetics, and the "this-is-really-fiction" books by ex–vice presidents, ex–presidential advisers, and ex-nannies of Princess Margaret. And there it is, one copy of your book, nestled between *Doris Day: Her Own Story*, by A. E. Hotchner and a book called *Is Film Film?* by an American university professor who also runs as a movie critic.

You look around to see if anyone is looking, then you

saunter over and pick up not your book at first, but one of the others. "Film," asks the professor-critic, "what is film? Is it only the isomorphous material from which the director molds his symbolic media message, or is it something more? Something *much* more?" He then goes on to say a lot of other things, but none as exciting, as stimulating, as that first riveting question, so you slide his book back on the shelf and concentrate on your book. If yours is a large book, it stands right out and seems to say, "Buy me. I'm more important than the smaller books around me." But if your book is only 5½ by 8¼ inches, it has a tendency to lower its eyes and slink back into the shadows of the big books, daring the book buyer (or even the author) to ferret it out. I picked up *Growing Up in Hollywood* casually, as though I were browsing, preoccupied, thinking about something else. The truth is, of course, that I *was* thinking of something else. My mind was on Art and the manager. I didn't want the manager to catch me trying to cover two hundred copies of *The Final Days* (7 by 9½ inches each) with one quivering copy of *Growing Up in Hollywood.*

As I looked over, my friend and the manager were walking toward me. The manager said, "It's right over here in the Film department." He was apparently going to show Art where he had hidden my book. I couldn't get it back in its place without being noticed, so as they arrived I said, "I see you're down to one copy of my book. Ha ha."

I don't know why I said "Ha ha." I'll never say it again to a bookseller. The manager said "Ha ha" back at me and then he said, "They all say that. Authors. Ha ha. They all notice how many of their books are on the shelf. Ha ha."

"I'll buy it," I said.

Art lit his already-lit cigar.

The manager said "Ha ha" again and then, "That will be ten forty-five, with tax." I gave him eleven dollars and he went off to the cash register.

"That's not the way for an author to make money," Art said. "What in the hell do you want a copy of your own book for?"

"I bought it for you," I lied.

"That's even jerkier than buying it for yourself," said my comforting friend. "Your publisher has already sent me a review copy."

"How'd you like it?" I said.

"What I've read so far is fine," he said.

I've noticed that authors' friends usually read only parts of books. Through a computer error at the publisher's, over a period of nine weeks nine copies of *Growing Up in Hollywood* were sent to the director of a film society, a friend of mine. Each time he got a copy he wrote me a note saying that he was "dipping into" *Growing Up in Hollywood,* as though it were some kind of guacamole or a cold swimming pool, and that he "liked what [he] had read so far." I met him at Dominick's Steak House on Beverly Boulevard in Los Angeles eight months after he got the last copy and he said, "I'm enjoying your book." I went home and looked at the date of his first letter. Then I divided the number of pages in the book by the number of days since he took his first dip, and it turned out that his average reading speed, so far, was three-tenths of a page a day, a statistic that makes an author nervous about the narrative drive of his book, to say nothing about the reading ability of the director of the film society.

The manager came back with my book, neatly wrapped, and gave me my change. "Ten forty-five," he said, then he handed me eleven nickels, one at a time. "Fifty, fifty-five, sixty, sixty-five, seventy, seventy-five, eighty, eighty-five, ninety, ninety-five, one hundred," he said. "That makes eleven dollars. Ha ha." He laughed as though they were the funniest nickels in the world.

"Bob says he'll be glad to do some autographing while he's here," said Art.

The manager stopped laughing and said, "That means we'll have to unwrap it."

"No," said Art. "Not that one. If he decides to autograph that one, he can do it after he gets back to the hotel. I thought you might like to have the rest of your copies autographed."

"That's it," said the bookseller. Then he remembered that he was really a hyena *posing* as a bookseller, so he added, "Ha ha."

"That's what?" said Art.

"That's the only one we have. Ha ha. That's our complete stock. Ha ha. The author bought our complete stock of his own book. Ha ha."

"Yeah, I guess he did," said Art. He turned to me. "Do you want to give it back?"

"Hell, no," I said. "I need this copy."

"What for?" said Art.

"I'll tell you later," I said.

The bookseller-hyena laughed again and said if he got another copy in and if I would leave my phone number, he would call me and I could come in and autograph it. Art thanked him for his courtesy and cooperation, and I thanked him for giggling at the funny nickels and gave him my London phone number.

"Just call this number and ask for the author of *Growing Up in Hollywood*," I said, "and I'll pop right over."

When we got out on the sidewalk, Art said, "Well, that's the general idea. It will probably vary from store to store, manager to manager, but that should give you a pretty good picture of what it's like for an author to promote his book personally."

"Do *you* go through this every time you write a book?" I asked. "Does Irwin Shaw? Does Gore Vidal? Does Solzhenitsyn?"

"Well," said Art, "not exactly. As I told you, it varies, depending on the bookseller, the author, where the book is on the *New York Times* best-seller list, things like that. For example, I've never done the rounds with Alex or Gore, but I've walked around with Irwin Shaw, and he usually just looks to see how many of his books are in the window. I've never seen him buy one of his own books at the retail price." He looked down at the copy of my book. "By the way," he said, "what *are* you going to do with that copy?"

"I'm going to send it to Irwin Shaw," I said.

"I thought he had read it," said Art.

"He has," I said, "but maybe he wants to read it again."

"Good idea," said Art. He looked at his watch. "I'd better be getting back to the office. I've got a column to get out. Now that you know the routine, why don't you work some of the other bookstores?"

"Yeah," I said. "Maybe I will. I want to walk around Washington anyway, see the old town. I haven't been back since Kathie and I were married here during the war."

"Well, Brentano's is on F Street, and there are a couple of bookstores on Fourteenth Street," he said. "The main thing is to introduce yourself to the manager and tell him the name of your book. If he hasn't got it in his store, he will at least have heard of it. If he does have it, try to restrain yourself from buying a copy. I don't think even Irwin Shaw would want to read it three times, not at ten bucks a shot."

"OK," I said. "Thanks a lot. I'll see you tonight."

I walked over to Brentano's and wandered around, but I couldn't find *Growing Up in Hollywood*. It's a big bookstore with a lot of clerks, and I couldn't tell which one was the manager. I asked a pimply-faced girl with thick, bifocal glasses for the book. She said she had never heard of it, but if I would give her the name of the publisher and the publication date she would check the catalogue. I gave her the information, and after a few minutes she came back smiling. She said the book wasn't listed in the publisher's catalogue under biography or nonfiction, but would I like her to look under gardening? I thanked her and told her that I was sure it wasn't under gardening. She said, "Well, I thought maybe 'growing up . . . ,' you know?" and I said, "Yes, I know, but I'm sure it's more about this little kid growing up in Hollywood than it is about vegetables and flowers growing up in Hollywood."

"What about *Vet in Harness?*"

"No," I said. "It's not about horses growing up in Hollywood, either."

She laughed and said, "No, I didn't mean that. I just thought you might be interested in some other book, and a number of customers have told me that *Vet in Harness* is very good, better than *Let Sleeping Vets Lie*."

"I'm sure it is," I said, "but I was only interested in that one book, *Growing Up in Hollywood*."

"If you'd like to leave your name and phone number, I'll call you if it comes in," she said.

"Art Buchwald," I said. "My name's Art Buchwald." She tipped her head back and looked at me through the bottom part of her bifocals. "I'm at the *Washington Post*," I added, and started for the door.

She followed me, and as I stepped out into the beautiful soft, spring sunshine, she said, "Goodbye, Mr. Buchwald."

I said, "Goodbye, and thank you," and she said, "Have a nice day," the way people do in America, even if it's raining.

18

Washington Interlude

During the war, Kathie and I had made an apartment out of the ballroom in the German embassy on 15th Street, and I thought I might go up and take a look at it. I was discouraged with my book-promotion tour and thought it might cheer me up to visit my old romantic haunts. I also wanted to see the little park at 14th and K streets where Kathie and I had courted. I was an apprentice seaman at the time and she was in the Red Cross, and the only place we could find any privacy was in this little park with three or four hundred other servicemen and Red Cross girls.

I walked to the park and sat on the bench that Kathie and I had sat on. The cherry trees were blooming all around, the weather was beautiful, and I closed my eyes and pretended it was 1943. The Russians had just opened a new offensive and pushed the Nazis back to the Dnieper. Sicily had fallen and Nazi paratroopers had spirited Mussolini out of Italy. The United States Fifth Fleet was pounding the Japanese in the South Pacific, and the Japanese were pounding back. Casualties were high, and Kathie and I were in Franklin Park on 14th Street and in love.

I remembered buying four T-shirts at the navy PX and spreading them on the park lawn thirty-three years ago, and as Kathie lay in my arms, we had talked about love and marriage and the second front that everyone kept saying was going to happen but that never did happen until the next year. While I was trying to recapture the exact moment that we had decided to make our lives together, a voice said, "Hey there, honey. My name's Audrey."

I opened my eyes and there sitting next to me on the sacred bench was a young woman. At first she could have passed as just another buck-toothed, overdressed, gum-chewing, black girl, carrying a patent-leather purse with a shoulder strap, wearing high-heeled patent-leather shoes, a short skirt, and too much makeup. But when she fluttered her false eyelashes and said, "How'd y'all like to try a little afternoon black stuff?," I knew there was more there than met the eye, or at least as much.

From time to time, during my long life, I have been propositioned by prostitutes, and I never quite know what to say without offending. When I was younger of course, it was easier. I just said, "OK, where?," or "OK, how much?" Now that I'm older, I find satisfactory answers harder to come by. I've tried "No, thank you" and "Why don't you get a decent job?" and "Do your parents know where you are?" and other variations on that theme, but none of them seems to work if the girl is really determined. They usually answer, "You don't really mean it, baby, let's go," or, "Look, man, don't gimme no lectures," or "Go to hell, old man," or something like that. Then I feel terrible.

In this case, and under the circumstances — my nostalgic mood and all — I decided to be polite, so I told Audrey it was nice of her, but that I wouldn't have time to sample any afternoon black stuff, or any afternoon white stuff either, for that matter, because I was just resting a few minutes on the way to an appointment with my skin doctor. I've found that most prostitutes think that "skin" means syphilis, which is something they're not too crazy about, and that if you drop it into the conversation early, they usually go on their merry way. Audrey was no exception. She said, "Bye, now," and moved off in a cloud of cheap perfume.

I closed my eyes again and tried to recapture the feeling of the past, but it didn't work. Audrey had come between me and that enchanting blue-eyed Red Cross girl of long ago. However, I kept my eyes closed and remembered how Kathie had stood up, and how I had loved her perfect legs and her pretty blonde hair and everything about her, and how we had folded the T-shirts and put them in a bag and decided not to get married until I had saved $10,000 out of my $33.40-per-month navy pay.

Another voice, not Audrey's, said, "Hello." I opened my eyes and there was another girl, a pretty one this time: soft skin, coffee-colored, with clear, straight eyes. "Lonely?" she said.

"What's your name?" I said.

"Thelma," she said. "My name's Thelma. Would you like to make love to me?"

"Here?" I said. "I don't think so. There's too much traffic. This must be the busiest bench in Washington."

She laughed, and she had pretty teeth. Her nose was the right size and in the right place, and the rest of her features all fit neatly together, but it was her eyes that kept me interested. They were pale blue, like those of some of the pretty Carib girls of Dutch descent that one sees from time to time in Trinidad and Tobago.

"No," she said. "Not here. We can go across the street to the Harrington."

In 1943 the Harrington had been a comfortable, very proper hotel where Kathie and I had first slept together. I had phoned and reserved the room two weeks ahead, and every time I passed the hotel during the two weeks' wait I felt guilty, sure that we would be caught, that I would be court-martialed, that Kathie would be drummed out of the Red Cross, and that the fat house detective, who would break into our room, would blackmail us for the rest of our lives.

When the fateful Saturday night finally came, I signed the register "Robert Parrish, U.S.N.R., and wife, R.C." We were in civilian clothes and the reception clerk asked what the letters were. He said he knew that U.S.N.R. stood for United States Navy Reserve, but what was R.C.? "My wife's a registered chiropodist," I said, and he told the bell captain to take "Mr. and Mrs. Parrish" to room 636. The bell captain did, and I overtipped him.

Kathie and I stayed in the big double bed in room 636 at the Harrington Hotel for thirty-six hours straight. It was there that we abandoned the idea of saving $10,000 before getting married. In fact, we were married two weeks later. I hadn't been back to the Harrington since, thirty-three years, and I didn't feel much like going there now with Thelma and her pale-blue eyes.

"No, Thelma," I said. "I really don't want to go to the Harrington Hotel with you."

"Why not?" she said.

"Sentimental reasons," I answered.

Her pale blues never blinked, never left my narrow greys. "I believe in sentimental reasons," she said. "What's in the package?"

"A book," I said. "A book I've already read. Would you like to have it?"

"What's it about?" she said.

"It's about movie stars," I said. It isn't, but I thought Thelma might be more interested in movie stars than in some unknown kid growing up in Hollywood, or anywhere else.

"Sure," she said. "Sure I'd like to have it." She smiled a little bit and then said, "I can read." I smiled back, and she smiled some more, and for a moment I almost played a return engagement at the Harrington, Red Cross or no Red Cross.

"OK," I said. "It's yours. If you get bored with it, just stop reading. Give it to someone else." As I handed her the book, a familiar voice, not mine and not Thelma's, said, "You're wasting your time, honey."

I looked up and saw my old friend Audrey. She was now carrying a sniveling Pekinese who was gasping for breath in the Washington heat.

"Hi, Audrey," said Thelma.

"I'm going over to the Harrington and get some food for Charlotte," said Audrey. "Wanta come with me?" She kissed the gasping, pug-nosed bitch full in the mouth and said, "Don't ums worry. Mama's gonna get ums some chopped-up Kansas City prime."

I am not a serious dog-hater. On the other hand, I am not a serious dog-lover. I can take most dogs or leave them, as long as they don't foul the new beige carpet in the hall or bark when I'm trying to sleep or bite my kids when they don't deserve it. The only breed I really can't bear is the Pekinese. (I confess to a narrow-minded prejudice here.) Another of my pet aversions (no pun intended, of course) is people who talk

to dogs as though they were people. I've been exposed to
quite a bit of this kind of thing and find that it doesn't make me
nauseated as long as it's limited to "Heel" or "Down, Fido" or
"Go get it, boy" when you throw a stick or one of those rubber
bones. But I've noticed that, like Audrey, some intelligent
people quite often resort to baby talk when talking to dogs,
even if the conversation is with a sixteen-year-old Pekinese
("Human equivalent: one hundred and twelve years," they
promptly tell you).

"Don't ums want ums' steak?" said Audrey.

Charlotte stuck out her wafer-thin pink tongue and let out a
wheezing sound that Audrey seemed to interpret as, "If you
don't mind, I'd prefer a loin lamb chop."

"What's that?" said Audrey. "Is ums tired of Kansas City
prime? Does ums want lamby-wamby this time?" (Imagine
talking like that to a 112-year-old.) Charlotte gasped again and
licked one of Audrey's lips, and I wondered if rabies could be
passed by kissing. Their lips finally parted and Audrey said,
"You comin', honey?" At first I thought she was still talking to
the 112-year-old bitch, but it turned out she was talking to
Thelma.

"Might as well," said Thelma. She stood up and held out
her hand to me. "Good luck," she said. "Thanks for the book."

"The same to you," I said. As they walked away I said, "The
same to both of you."

They both waved without looking back.

A block north of Franklin Park, on the opposite side of 14th
Street, there is a bookstore with a sign over the door that says
WASHINGTON'S LARGEST BOOKSTORE. I decided to go in and
meet the manager and make my pitch. As soon as I walked in I
knew it wasn't my kind of bookstore. Hanging on the wall, on
the left, were two life-sized pink inflated nude rubber figures,
one male and one female. I know there are a lot of jokes these
unisex days about how it's difficult to tell the difference, but
there was no problem here. The female's legs were spread
open in the conventional copulation position and the rubber
gentleman had an erection. They were each holding strings
with colored balloons on the ends (pink for the lady, blue for
the gentleman). On the lady's pink balloon was painted "Take

me home for $88.75," and on the gentleman's blue balloon was painted "Take me home for $89.50." I never did find out why the male was more expensive.

There were several attendants in the store, some black, some white, all rather neatly dressed. A black fellow behind the aphrodisiac counter said, "May I help you, sir?"

"Well, yes," I said. "Do you have a book called *Growing Up in Hollywood?*" (What did I have to lose?)

"Hard or soft," he said.

"Hardback," I said. "Published by Harcourt Brace Jovanovich."

"No, I meant hard core or soft core."

"Oh, well," I said. "It's not really a pornographic book. I mean, core-wise, it's, well . . . it's . . . it's not a core book either. It's more of a straight biography." He didn't say anything, so I said, "I don't have anything against pornographic books, but the one I'm asking about just doesn't happen to be one." He remained silent, so I said, "I mean, it *is* a book, but it's not pornographic."

"Every honest book is pornographic," he said. "Sex is universal."

"Yes," I said. "*Growing Up in Hollywood* is mostly about kids."

He looked at me patiently for a few moments and then said, "That's when it all starts."

"What starts?" I said.

"Sex," he said. "You're born with it. Why don't you just browse around for a few minutes. I'll look in our catalogue under teenage sex, masturbation, and related subjects."

"Well," I said. "I don't want to put you to any trouble. I mean, I don't want you plowing through your masturbation catalogue just for me."

"No trouble at all," he said. "Who's the author?"

"Art Buchwald," I said.

He looked at me again for what seemed like too long and then said, "Right. Make yourself at home. Look at a movie, it's only twenty-five cents. I won't be long."

After he left I wandered over to a little booth, walked in, and closed the door. There was a sign that said "This establishment is patrolled by the police regularly. Not more than one person to a booth. No urinating, etc." I didn't feel like urinating, etc., and even if I had, I would have restrained myself because I didn't want any trouble with the law. I put a quarter in the slot, the lights went out, and there in front of me, in color, was a very pretty white girl practicing oral sex on a muscular black gentleman. Perhaps practicing isn't the correct word. This seemed to be an actual performance, enhanced by a scratchy sound track of *oh*'s and *ah*'s and *slip-it-to-me-baby*'s and *aaarrrggghhh!!*'s. At the crucial moment, just when the performers seemed to be arriving at some kind of climax, the leading lady interrupted her performance, turned to the camera, and gasped, "Put another quarter in — *please!*" and the screen went black. The sound track, however, continued with heavy breathing and both performers yelling "Oh, my God" and "Please don't stop" and "Now, baby." I fumbled in my pocket for another quarter and the lady performer screamed, *"Now! For God's sake! Now!"* I put the quarter in as fast as I could and the goddamn film started again at the beginning.

I stepped out of the booth, and the salesman told me that he couldn't find *Growing Up in Hollywood* in his catalogue, that perhaps I would like some other book. I demurred, but he said, "Why don't you at least take a look. Most of the better ones are over there in the back, behind the dildo display." I thanked him and explained that I was in a bit of a hurry, that I was only in town one day, and that I was actually on a nostalgia trip to my honeymoon haunts of thirty-three years ago. He was most sympathetic, and as I walked out past the two nude balloons, he, too, said, "Have a nice day."

What was once our honeymoon apartment at 1221 15th Street NW is now a parking lot. Fifteenth used to be a quiet, residential street. Now, it is a one-way, through-traffic artery, going north, and if you want to park in what used to be our living room, you must get on the right side as you cross Massachusetts Avenue, start your right-turn indicator two blocks ahead, and hope that you don't wind up in court with a whiplash lawsuit. The traffic is frightening. There is a Holiday Inn across the street on Rhode Island Avenue and a modern glass-and-steel building, which is the home of the American Association for the Advancement of Science, diagonally across at 1515 Massachusetts Avenue.

The only original building left in the block is number 1325. Fourteen steps lead up to the front porch, and as I passed, a Chinese woman in a coolie outfit and an attractive young black girl were trying to get a double mattress up the steps. They were laughing good-naturedly as the unwieldy mass slid down to the sidewalk each time they got it about halfway up the steps. Despite my arthritic shoulder, I offered to help them. They accepted my offer, and we were soon all three laughing as we struggled ineffectually with the mattress. I somehow managed to get under it and was edging up the steps like a turd-tumbler beetle carrying a horseapple, when the black girl said, "Hold it." I stopped, gratefully, and tried to recover my breath. I peeked out and saw that a giant beer-delivery truck had stopped in front of the house.

The traffic screeched to a stop behind the truck and the horns started to blow and the motorists started to curse. The driver took a sign out of the cab and hung it on the back of his truck. "The driver regrets any inconvenience caused while he is delivering Michelob, Washington's finest beer," said the sign. As the cursing increased and the horns blew louder, the burly driver gave the motorists the old middle finger and sauntered over to the steps.

"Need any help?" he asked.

The Chinese woman giggled and the pretty black girl said, "Help is what we need the most."

"Who's under the mattress?" said the truck driver.

"Another one of our volunteers," said the girl.

The truck driver walked up to where he thought my head might be and tapped the mattress. "Let me handle it, Mac," he said.

I craned out and got a good look at him for the first time. He had tattoos on both arms and was smoking something that looked and smelled more like a lamp wick than a cigar. I don't like to be called Mac, especially when I'm wearing a double mattress on a very hot day, but this fellow weighed at least two hundred pounds, and he seemed to know what he was talking about, so I scrambled out from under the mattress and let it slide back down to the sidewalk for the eighth time. The Chinese woman giggled louder than ever, and the truck driver, whose name turned out to be Romeo ("I'm Armenian, not Italian"), said, "Where's it supposed to go?"

"Right up to the top," said the pretty black girl. Her name was Lucille.

Romeo looked up to the top floor, then at the mattress, then back over to Lucille. "OK," he said. He went to the cab of his truck and got two pieces of rope. The traffic jam in back of his truck was now worse than ever. A particularly irate driver in a Mercedes shook his fist at Romeo and yelled, "I'll never drink Michelob again, you bastard." Romeo smiled and took a deep Shakespearean bow. The driver laughed in spite of himself.

Romeo had apparently had some previous experience with mattresses. He folded our troublesome, lumpy mess like a crepe suzette, tied the ends, and worked it onto his back, where he held it with one arm. He turned to the Chinese woman and said, "You go ahead of us, Mama San. See that all the doors are open." Mama San padded obediently up the steps and opened the front door. "You stay close to me, honey," he said to Lucille, "and you, Mac," — he pointed his smoldering wick at me — "you bring up the rear." He took over the whole operation as though it were his right and his duty. He reminded me of a sergeant Bushinsky I had known in the Ninth Armored Division. Bushinsky had also called me Mac and he had managed to put a pontoon bridge across the Rhine under enemy fire in March 1945 when the swollen river was flowing at nine knots. It all worked because the rest of us recognized a born leader and did exactly as we were told.

"Right," I said to Romeo. I almost said, "Yes, sir," not sarcastically, but because he seemed to rate it.

"OK," said Romeo, "let's go. Keep a tight formation." He led the way up the steps and into the hall. Mama San ran ahead, Lucille kept her position beside Romeo, and I stopped to close the front door. I looked out and the Mercedes driver was standing behind Romeo's truck, taking his license number. When I looked back around, Romeo and Lucille were halfway up the first flight of stairs and Romeo had his free hand on Lucille's miniskirted bottom.

On the second floor, a blonde wearing a robe came out of the bathroom carrying a basin and a towel. "Hi, Lucille," she said, as our procession passed.

"Hello, honey," said Lucille.

The blonde looked at the mattress and then at me tagging along behind. "That's what I call an eager customer," she said.

Lucille laughed. Romeo's muffled voice said, "Come on, baby," and our caravan started up the last flight of stairs.

Lucille's room was bright and airy and completely unfurnished except for a double brass bed and a sink with a towel hanging on a rack under it. Romeo dumped the mattress on the bed and fell on top of it. The legs gave way and Lucille and Mama San laughed hysterically as Romeo rolled off onto the floor.

The noise from the street was almost deafening. Police sirens were now mixing with the horns. Romeo went to the window and looked down. He turned back, pointed to the bed, and said to me, "See if you can put it together, Mac. I'll be back in a minute." He patted Lucille on the bottom on the way out and said, "Don't let it cool off, baby."

Lucille, Mama San, and I got the legs back on the bed and the mattress in place. We went to the window and looked down. The traffic was now backed up behind Romeo's truck all the way to Massachusetts Avenue, and we could see Romeo waving his tattooed arms and explaining the situation to four policemen, two from the squad car and two on motorcycles. We couldn't hear what he was saying, what with the horns and sirens and screaming motorists. It turns out that Washington police cars continue blasting out a terrifying, undulating sound long after they arrive at the scene of a crime. I think it's supposed to intimidate the criminal, keep him on the defensive, and deafen him. A giant motorcycle cop yelled something to Romeo and Romeo yelled back at him. The cop pointed to Romeo's truck and Romeo pointed up to us. The cop didn't even look up, he just kept pointing to the truck and yelling. Finally, Romeo shrugged and looked up and waved to us. Lucille blew him a kiss, and we all waved back and laughed as Romeo climbed into the cab of his truck. Mama San left the room discreetly and closed the door. As the noise from outside diminished, Lucille and I sat on the bed and laughed some more at Romeo.

"He was awfully nice to offer to carry the mattress up for us," she said. "I'm sorry I didn't get a chance to thank him properly."

"I offered to carry it up first," I said. "You can thank me properly."

Lucille laughed and then got up and lowered the shade, and I lay back on the bed. She went over and ran some cold water on the towel and held it on her soft brown throat for a moment, then she sat on the side of the bed and put the cool towel on my brow. It smelled of her and her perfume, and I closed my eyes. Lucille said, "Thank you properly." I suddenly felt that everything was going to be all right, which it was, up to a point. The point that everything stopped being all right was when Lucille got up to lock the door. "What do you suppose Romeo was telling the cops?" she said. She was reaching for the latch when the door burst open, and there was Romeo with eight six-packs of Michelob and a transistor radio.

"I told 'em I had to finish my delivery," he said. "It's OK to park as long as I'm making deliveries." He turned the Animals singing "The House of the Rising Sun" up to eardrum capacity. "I gave each cop a six-pack and they're watching the truck for me," he said. He kissed Lucille on the cheek, then barged into the room, followed by Mama San and the blonde from the second floor. The blonde was now wearing a blue cotton dress and nothing else except some earrings and a toothy grin. Romeo tossed six cans of beer on the bed and said, "Come on, Mac. Open 'em up. It's party time."

His voice still carried quite a bit of authority, so I opened the beer and we each drank some and laughed at the cops and the traffic and the mattress. It was all very friendly, but somehow it wasn't the same as before Romeo had come back with Mama San and the gaddamn blonde, whose name was Madeline and who kept saying, "I've got a nicer room than this on the second floor," while Mama San grinned approval. Lucille was asking Romeo about the tattoos on his arms, and he was telling her about them and hinting that the real good ones were hidden away, and that if Lucille said the magic words, he might be willing to show them to her.

Lucille said, "Where are they?"

Romeo said, "That's it! Those are the magic words! You got 'em the first time!" He started to unbutton his shirt, and when

I saw the word *Mother* tattooed on his left breast, just above his Armenian nipple, I decided it was time to leave.

"I'd better be getting along," I said.

"I got that one in Singapore," said Romeo.

"I'm supposed to meet some people at the South Agriculture building," I said. "I don't want to be late."

Lucille and Madeline were now helping Romeo disrobe, admiring the artwork as each tattoo was disclosed. "What's '*semper fidelis*'?" said Madeline.

"Marine Corps," said Romeo. "Means 'always faithful.' Had it done in Manila."

"Thanks for the beer," I said.

"Be my guest," said Romeo.

"What's 'Don't tread on me'?" said Lucille.

"American history," said Romeo. "Flag of the thirteen colonies. Remember?"

I stopped at the door and shook hands with Mama San, who smiled politely and bowed. I was through the door and halfway down the stairs when I heard Romeo say, "Where in the hell did my old buddy, Mac, go?"

Down on 15th Street the traffic was flowing smoothly: three policemen were directing it around the Michelob truck. As I passed on my way to Thomas Circle, the policeman nearest the curb said, "Have a nice day," just as the girl in Brentano's and the book salesman in Washington's largest book store had done earlier in the afternoon.

Massachusetts Avenue now runs under Thomas Circle, but the circle itself is still the intersection for Vermont Avenue, 14th Street, and M Street. There are sixteen traffic signals around the circle, and to the uninitiated, they all seem to be flashing WALK and DON'T WALK at the same time. As I approached the circle, a curly-haired teenager touched my arm and asked me for fifty cents. I asked him what it was for and he said it was for His Divine Grace, A. C. Bhaktivedanta Swami Prabhupada.

"Who is he?" I asked politely.

"Swami Prabhupada is the Founder-Acarya of the International Society for Krishna Consciousness," said the teenager. "It is through him that you will meet the Lord."

I have a certain respect for all religions, so I told this kid to piss off, that I didn't even know His Divine Grace, and if I did, I'd tell him to get off his ass and work for a living instead of sending kids out to beg for him. I walked away as fast as I could, but my arthritis had come back a bit and the little bastard kept right up with me, hocking me a lot of static and chanting "*Hare Krishna*," which, in his opinion, he said, is the sublime method for reviving our transcendental consciousness. We came to the corner and the flashing lights told me that I couldn't go in any direction. At least fifty lights kept blinking DON'T WALK, so I stood there helpless while this jerk told me that by chanting this maha mantra, I could perceive a transcendental ecstasy coming through from the spiritual stratum. When I looked away from him, he segued into instructions for chanting: "Begin with meditation beads next to shaved head." I pointed out that *his* head was not shaved, and without pausing he said that in addition to the fifty cents for His Divine Grace, A. C. Bhaktivedanta Swami Prabhupada, would I like to give him seventy-five cents to get his head shaved? Since I had already told him, with no effect, to piss off, this time I just said, "I like it better the way it is."

"Do you?" he said. "I mean, do you really like my hair better this way?"

"I like it better that way than giving you a handout to get it shaved off," I said.

"How about an afro?" he said.

Fortunately, the flashing red DON'T WALK signs changed to flashing green WALK signs and I dutifully started to walk across the street. The Hare Krishna disciple had apparently reached his territorial limit because he stood there, sadly, and watched me go, another lost soul. Me, not him. When I got to the traffic island in the middle of Vermont Avenue, I looked back and he was still standing there, forlornly. The flashing signals were urging me to walk some more, so I crossed back over and gave the poor sonofabitch fifty cents, and he gave me, in return, a little paperback book titled *On Chanting Hare Krishna* by His Divine Grace A. C. Bhaktivedanta Swami Prabhupada. I turned to make my escape, but the DON'T WALK signs were now threatening me again, so I hailed a cab. As I hurried to the cab, the teenager yelled, "What about the haircut?" I

closed the cab door and leaned out of the window. The teenager ran over, and when he was up close I said, "Go for the
afro, kid. It'll look great on you." Then I told the driver to take
me to the Madison Hotel and rolled up the window before
Bhaktivedanta Swami Prabhupada's disciple could tell me to
have a nice day.

As I walked into my room at the Madison, the phone was
ringing. I didn't feel much like talking to anybody, but I an-
swered it anyway. It was Buchwald. "How'd it go?" he said.
   "Not bad, I guess."
   "Did you sell any books?"
   "Well, no. Not exactly."
   There was a pause. I could hear Art striking a match and
lighting his cigar. Finally he said, "Did you *buy* any more
books?"
   My eye fell on *On Chanting Hare Krishna* by His Divine
Grace, A. C. Bhaktivedanta Swami Prabhupada. "Yes, as a
matter of fact I did," I said. "I bought one more book after I
left you."
   "I knew I should have gone with you," said Art.
   "I wish you had," I said.
   "How was the trip down memory lane?" he said. "How was
the old nostalgia cruise down Fourteenth Street?"
   "Interesting," I said. "But the neighborhood has changed a
lot. It's not at all as I remember it."
   "That's because you're now looking at it through an author's
eyes," he said. "It's bound to look different. Before, you were
a pea-green twenty-two-year-old sailor, not even dry behind
the ears. Did you ever think of it that way?"
   "Well, not really," I said. "Not at the time. I mean, Kathie
was there then, and she was young too, and I don't remember
looking behind her ears for dampness or anything like that. I
just remember being in love with her, and lying on these
T-shirts in Franklin Park, and taking her to the Harrington
and —"
   "You took your wife to the Harrington?" Art said. "The
Harrington Hotel on Fourteenth Street?"
   "She wasn't my wife at the time," I defended. "She was a
Red Cross girl."

"Oh, I see," said my friend. His tone made it sound as though it was all right for the woman I have been married to for thirty-three years to work in a brothel on 14th Street, as long as she was in the Red Cross.

"The Harrington was different then," I said. "It wasn't a place where you could take some hooker and get laid. It was a very respectable hotel." There was no reply so I said, "Hello, operator?"

"No, I'm here," said Art. "I was just thinking about what you said. About how you couldn't get laid in the Harrington Hotel on Fourteenth Street in nineteen forty-three."

"That isn't what I said," I said.

Another pause. Then, "What *did* you say?"

"I just said that things are different now."

"Of course they're different, but so are you. You are now a sophisticated man of the world, an artist. You've just had a book published. You can see and appreciate things as they really are, not just as you want them to be. That's why Edward Bennett Williams said it's so much fun to be a writer."

It was my turn to pause. Art said, "Hello, Bob?"

"Yes," I said. "I'm here."

"Well, what do you think?" he said.

"About what?"

"About being a writer."

"I think Edward Bennett Williams was probably right," I said. "Writers do meet a lot of interesting people."

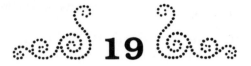

19

"Swifty" Lazar, the Talk Shows, and How to Saw an Author in Half

The literary agent for my book was Irving Paul Lazar, the same agent who negotiated our *In the French Style* deal. He is known far and wide — and in some places affectionately — as "Swifty," but though he is a treasured friend of long standing, I still address him as Irving. "Swifty" always seemed inappropriate for so peculiarly talented a man. Now that he numbers a former president of the United States among his clients, it might even seem disrespectful.

Lazar operates from a modest office on South Beverly Drive in Beverly Hills. He has two secretaries and a speaker on his phone that broadcasts the voice on the other end like the public-address systems in airports. This permits Irving to carry on with his work during a phone conversation without having to hold the phone. It also permits his visitors to hear every word that's said at both ends. His office is crowded with books, manuscripts, and inscribed photographs of his famous friends and clients, dead and alive. John Kennedy, Cole Porter, Moss Hart, and Ernest Hemingway represented the former group at the time of my author tour. Irwin Shaw, Peter Viertel, Lauren Bacall, Henry Kissinger, and Lazar himself were some of the live ones. In one picture, Lazar is facing a cow at a *tienta* in Spain. He is aiming the muleta at the cow and looking back over his shoulder at his host, Luis Miguel Dominguin, one of the greatest bullfighters of his day. Irving is short and bald. He wears thick bifocals and he doesn't look

like a classic matador. The cow in the photograph is also looking at Luis Miguel with a bewildered look on its face.

"No problem with Johnny Carson," said Irving. "I gave the
book to Freddie and he loved it. Couldn't put it down. His
wife liked it too."

"Great," I said. "Who's Freddie?"

"Freddie deCordova," said Irving. "He produces the
Johnny Carson show. This is a great break. We'll sell five
thousand copies just by having the book on Carson. It's the top
show on the air."

"What kind of questions will Johnny Carson ask me?"

"Johnny won't be on the show himself the night you're on,"
said Irving. "He's on vacation. Orson Welles will be the guest
host. That'll be better for us because Orson knows a lot about
old movies. Fits in with the subject of our book."

Lazar has a comforting way of making you feel that he is on
your side. It's always "us" and "we" and "our," never "you"
nor "I" nor "yours" nor "mine." When my book finally appeared, Lazar promptly marched in and bought ten copies at
Doubleday's, one of the largest bookstores in Beverly Hills.
He then persuaded the manager to put his remaining five
copies in the window, next to *Nightwork* by Irwin Shaw, another client.

"When you sell those," he said, "I'll bring the author in and
get him to autograph your new supply." I was standing beside
him and could have autographed the five books in the window
right then, but when I reached for my pen, Lazar said, "Later,
not now. Let him sell those first."

Two days before the Johnny Carson show, Lazar called and
said he had to see me. He said it was urgent. "I'll be right
over," I said.

"I may as well give it to you straight," Lazar said when I
walked into his office.

"Relax, Irving," I said. "I've been on this bookselling tour
for ten days now. Nothing's going to surprise me, not even if
you give it to me crooked. Tell me what's on your mind."

"OK, here it is, straight from the shoulder." I glanced down
at his well-tailored shoulder. "Orson doesn't want you on the
show," he said.

I had worked at RKO when Welles made *Citizen Kane,* and years later I had directed him in *Casino Royale.* We were friends.

"Why not?" I asked.

"He won't be on any program where they talk about old movies. He says he's tired of the past and is looking to the future."

"What does he see in the future?" I said.

"Magic," said Irving. "Orson's interested in magic, conjuring tricks. That's what he wants to talk about on the program. He says he's afraid if he introduces a book about Hollywood, it will identify him with *Citizen Kane!*"

In my opinion *Citizen Kane* is one of the best movies ever made, but if Welles wanted the world to forget that he made it, I was prepared to go along with him.

"Where is Orson?" I said. "Maybe I should talk to him."

"You can't," said Irving. "He won't give out his number. We may as well face it, the guy's trying to create a new image for himself. He wants to be a fat Houdini."

"Well, when you see him, tell him he just sawed a friend in half."

"Don't take it personally. Orson says you can be on the show if you can do some card tricks or something. If not, they've got Buddy Hackett standing by. Freddie deCordova says Orson is adamant."

I had seen Orson adamant a few times when we were making *Casino Royale,* and it had never been a pretty sight.

"OK," I said, "if Freddie manages to get through to Orson, tell him I think he should go with Buddy Hackett. Tell him I hear Buddy's got some voodoo jokes."

"Don't worry about it," said my philosophical agent.

"I won't if you won't. It's only five thousand books. You can go into Doubleday's and buy that many on your lunch hour tomorrow. Does Freddie know about this?"

"Freddie who?" said Irving.

"Freddie the producer," I said. "Freddie who couldn't put my book down. Freddie whose wife liked it too. Freddie the producer of the Johnny Carson show."

"Forget the Carson show. That's not what I wanted to talk to you about. His show's not so hot anyway. I think it's been slipping."

I didn't have the heart to remind him that in three days Carson had gone from "the top show on the air" to "not so hot." I tried to think of something to cheer him up and finally said, "What about Merv Griffin? Does his show sell books?"

"That's really why I wanted to see you," said Irving. "I called Merv's producer this morning. Woke him up. He says he'll put you on as a favor to me."

"Well, what the hell, what's wrong with that? What if it is second best? Suppose we only sell *four* thousand books."

"There's a slight problem." I looked at Irving's shoulder again, waiting for him to give me more bad news straight from it. Instead he sat down and aged twenty years. There was a crack of thunder outside, unusual in Southern California.

I sat down next to the best agent in the business and said, "OK. What's the slight problem? What do I have to do to get on *The Merv Griffin Show*?"

"He wants you to deliver a major star. The producer says you're not famous enough."

"Oh."

"He says you can be on the show and plug your book if you get a star to appear with you. I told him that was no problem, that you had lots of friends in the business."

"How about Ronald Colman?" I said.

"Don't make jokes. Ronald Colman's dead."

"So why did you tell the guy there was no problem? Did the producer say it had to be a live star?" I said. "If he hangs a lot of restrictions on us, it's going to narrow the field. What are the guidelines? Who do they consider an acceptable star?"

"Jack Lemmon," said Irving. "They've been trying to get Lemmon on the show, and I suggested this might be a good opportunity. I told them you and Lemmon were friends, that you had directed him in a movie. I'm sure Jack wouldn't mind. It's good media exposure for him."

"Media exposure is not Jack Lemmon's problem these days," I said. "Besides, I hate to ask friends for favors."

"Do you hate to sell books?" said Irving.

"How the hell do I know? I haven't sold any yet."

"Call Lemmon. Tell him the situation. He can say no if he doesn't want to do it."

I called Lemmon and said, "What are you up to?"

"Oh," he said, "I was just lying here asleep, hoping that the phone wouldn't ring until summer. Who is that?"

"Bob Parrish," I said. I had forgotten that it was still early morning. "I want you to do me a favor."

"Anything you say, baby," he said. "Just let me get my sleeping mask off and vomit and I'll call you right back. What's your number?" I gave it to him and watched some color come back into Irving's cheeks.

"Merv'll really appreciate this," he said.

The phone rang and Lemmon's voice said, "Now, what's on your mind?"

"Selling books."

"I'll take ten."

"No," I said, "it's not just *any* book. I'm not a regular book salesman. I'm still a movie director. This just happens to be a book that I wrote myself."

"In that case I'll take twenty."

"Be serious."

"I'm always serious at eight forty-five in the morning after shooting all night on the Warner back lot."

"Well, here's the situation," I said. "Im trying to get on television to plug this book, and they won't let me on unless I bring along a major star."

"Now you're talking," said Lemmon. "What's the show and when's it on?"

"It's *The Merv Griffin Show* next week."

"Now you're not," he said.

"What do you mean?"

"*The Merv Griffin Show* next week," he said. My face must have fallen, over the phone, because he went on, "Gee, Bob baby, if there's any show on earth that I would love to do, it's Merv's. But unfortunately I'm off to the Alaskan tundra on an eight months' schedule tomorrow morning. Damn."

"That's just what I was going to say."

"What?"

"Damn."

"How's Kathie?"

"Fine. She's in China. How's Felicia?"

"I don't know. Wait a minute, I'll ask her." Through the phone I heard him say, "Farfel, Bob Parrish wants to know how you are. Kathie's in China." I didn't hear her answer, but Lemmon came back on and said, "She's fine. Says she's glad you called."

"Did she really say that?"

"She said something about your calling. Maybe it wasn't 'glad.' Maybe all she said was 'What time is it?' You know how women are in the morning."

"Yeah, well, give her my love."

"You bet. Let's get together before you leave."

"Anytime."

"Did you say China, that Kathie's in China?"

"That's right, China."

There was a pause and then he said, "I'll call you," and hung up.

"How did you do?" Irving asked.

"Zero. He says he'll be out of town."

"What other stars do you know? Weren't Mitchum and Rita Hayworth in the movie you directed with Lemmon?"

"Yes," I said, "but I'm not sure they would want to go on a television show for nothing when they make over $500,000 a picture. You see, these people are high-priced performers just like Merv Griffin and Johnny Carson, and they probably resent being on a nationally televised network program for the Equity minimum when Griffin and Carson are getting much more. They feel used. They don't want to do it unless they're plugging one of their own movies."

"Do you have Mitchum's number?"

"Have you ever called Bob Mitchum before noon when he's not working?"

"No, not really," said Irving.

"It can be very dangerous."

"How can he hurt you over the phone?"

"It isn't me. It's the people in his house. Maids and cooks and children and wives. People like that."

"How about his answering service? He must have an answering service. Call and leave a message."

"I wish I had thought of that with Lemmon," I said. It

started to rain, and Irving went over and looked gloomily out of the window. "It's unfair," he said.

"Come on, Irving, cut it out. I know you're trying to help me sell some books and I appreciate it, I really do. But it's embarrassing for me to call these guys. They're personal friends. So let's cut out the 'unfair' crap."

"I didn't mean that," he said. "I meant it's unfair that you've written a book, gotten good reviews, and I can't get you on a TV show unless you can do card tricks or bring a famous friend. I feel lousy about it."

I looked at the sad figure silhouetted against the rainy window. The shoulders that he gave bad news from sagged and he looked dispirited, even from the back. I swallowed some pride and dialed Mitchum's answering service. The girl said he was out of town and would return late that night. Irving suggested leaving a copy of my book at his house with a note. I agreed, and Irving said, "I'm sorry to ask you to go through this, Bob, but I really believe in your book and I want to put it over."

"Forget it," I said. "I'll get the book to Mitchum's house. Maybe he'll surprise us. He's a very unpredictable fellow."

"Let's keep our fingers crossed," said Irving. "What about John Wayne?" His promotional adrenaline was flowing again.

"What about him?"

"Well, he's a star, and you mention him in your book. Why don't you ask him to go on *The Merv Griffin Show* with you and Mitchum?"

"We haven't got Mitchum yet, Irving," I said, "and I haven't seen John Wayne in twenty years. I sent him a copy of the book and he never acknowledged it. If I call him, he'll say, 'Bob who?' Even his answering service would say, 'Bob who?'"

"I guess you're right," said Irving. "Let's concentrate on Mitchum." I sent the book to Mitchum's house with a note asking him to be on *The Merv Griffin Show* with me.

The next morning at 6:30 my doorbell rang and there was Mitchum. "I can't go on that show," he said. "I don't have a thing to wear." I ordered some breakfast and looked across at my old friend.

"It's a rip-off," he said. "They sell the time for fifty thousand dollars a minute because I, or some other clown, say we'll appear for nothing. The network sells some cornflakes, I make a jerk of myself, and Merv Griffin buys himself a new Learjet. I don't do 'em anymore."

"How's Dottie?" I said. Dottie is Mitchum's wife, a wonderful woman.

"Fine. She's reading your book. How's Kathie?"

"OK, I guess. She's in China."

"We've got to get together before you go home."

"Anytime."

"What's Kathie doing in China?"

"Just looking around," I said. "She hasn't been there for a while and there have been a lot of changes."

"When was she there last?"

"Nineteen thirty-nine," I said.

"Yeah," he said. "There've been a lot of changes." He looked at me for a moment, then said, "I can see why she'd want to check up from time to time." He finished his coffee and said. "You got any mescal around here?"

"No," I said. "But I've got some Scotch. It's not bad in the morning. I tried some yesterday at about this time."

"No, thanks," said Mitchum. "It's not the same. Mescal keeps me regular. Scotch keeps me drunk." He got up and put on his windbreaker. "I'm going home and take a nap," he said.

"At eight o'clock in the morning?"

"That's when I get my best sleep." He started for the door. "Take it easy, Rob," he said.

"Thanks for coming over."

"*De nada,*" he said. "I'll call ya." He slid through the door like a sleepy panther. When he was halfway down the stairs, he said, "*Hasta la vista,*" without looking back. One of the pictures we had made together had been shot in Mexico.

20

John Wayne
and
How to Sell Books in Chicago

The Hollywood Filmograph, April 26, 1930:

> John Ford has recommended a college boy, Marion
> "Duke" Morrison, to Raoul Walsh to play the leading role
> in Fox Studios' *The Big Trail.* . . . I can't see how anybody
> could stretch their imagination so far as to gamble
> $2,000,000 on a novice to make good in a picture that cries
> for an actor with years and years of experience. . . .

Raoul Walsh's Answer:

> I selected Morrison, whose name, by the way, will be
> John Wayne from now on, to play the Scout in *The Big
> Trail,* primarily because he is a real pioneer type, . . . but
> most of all because he can start over any trail and finish.

"Get me Irv Kupcinet in Chicago," yelled Irving Lazar. His
secretaries work in two small offices down the hall. I suppose
he could reach them on the intercom, but I have never seen
him use it.

"Don't worry about Merv Griffin," he said to me. "Kup'll
sell more books for us than Johnny Carson and Merv Griffin
combined." My fast-moving ebullient agent put Merv Griffin
out of his mind and behind him.

The secretary's voice said, "Mr. Kupcinet on two."

Lazar flipped the switch on his speaker phone and said,
"Hello, Kup, how are you?"

A Godlike voice said, "Hello, Swifty. How's the weather
out there?"

Leroy "Satchel" Paige and author, *The Wonderful Country*,
Durango, Mexico, 1958.

Tom Lea, author of *The Wonderful Country*, and Robert Mitchum.

Robert Mitchum and author, *The Wonderful Country*.

Author and Irwin Shaw, Place des Vosges, Paris, 1962.

Author and Jean Seberg, *In the French Style*, Paris, 1962.

Models, author, Jean Seberg, and Irwin Shaw on the first day
of shooting *In the French Style*.

Jean Seberg, *In the French Style.*

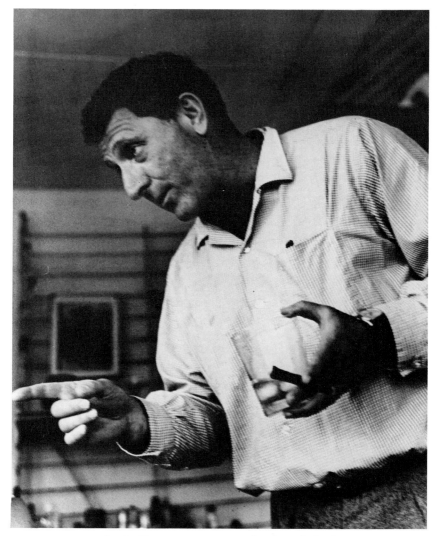

Irwin Shaw in action, *In the French Style*.

Orson Welles and author, *Casino Royale*, London, 1965.

Author, Ursula Andress, and Peter Sellers, *Casino Royale*.

Author and Ursula Andress, *Casino Royale*.

Britt Ekland and author, *The Bobo*, Barcelona, 1967.

Peter Sellers "knifing" author in the back, *The Bobo*.

Author, Cliff Robertson, Elmo Williams, and Darryl Zanuck,
Up From the Beach, Normandy, 1965.

Author, Darryl Zanuck, and Michel Wyn, *Up From the Beach*.

Author and James Coburn, *Duffy*, Almería, Spain, 1968.

Promotional poster for *A Town Called Bastard*, directed
by author in 1971 and released in both the U.S. and Spain.

Michael Caine, script supervisor, author, and Anthony Quinn,
The Marseilles Contract, Paris, 1974.

Pierre Salinger, Anthony Quinn, author, and James Jones,
The Marseilles Contract, Paris.

Author, James Mason, and Charles Millot,
The Marseilles Contract, Antibes.

Anthony Quinn and author, *The Marseilles Contract*, Marseilles.

The Swiss garage sale, Klosters, Switzerland, 1980.

"Terrible," said Irving. "Look, Kup, you've done a lot of favors for me in the past and now I'm gonna do one for you."

"I could use a favor," said the voice. "What is it, a horse in the Derby?"

"No, it's an author," said Irving. "Bob Parrish has written a delightful book which you're going to love."

"Bob who?" said the voice.

"Bob Parrish, the director. He's a great friend of mine as well as a client, and I want you to put him on your show. You won't regret it."

"Is that the favor?"

"Bob's with me now," said Irving. "He's going to New York for the *Today* show and I'd like him to stop off in Chicago. When do you tape your show?"

"Fridays," said the voice.

"Great," said Irving. "I'll have Bob on a plane tonight."

"Let me look into it," said the voice. "We're pretty crowded, but I'll do what I can. I'll get back to you."

"Who's on your show tomorrow night?" said Irving.

"John Wayne. He's coming in to plug *The Shootist*."

"Perfect," said Irving. His secretary came in and put some letters on his desk. Up until now he had been wandering around the room as he talked. Now, he sat down at his desk and started to read the letters through his half-moon glasses. "Hello, Kup. What do you think?"

"I'm thinking."

"Bob's book is *about* John Wayne," said Irving.

Wayne is mentioned in my book, but to say that the book is about him is like saying *Hamlet* is about two gravediggers. If the book is "about" anybody, it's about John Ford, the film director who discovered John Wayne and directed Wayne's best films.

"Christ, it's perfect," said Irving. He started to sign the letters.

"When's Parrish going to be on the *Today* show?" said the voice.

"It doesn't matter," said Irving. "We'll fit it in with you."

He knew, of course, that my publisher had been trying, desperately, to get me on the *Today* show and had so far been unsuccessful.

"I'll see if I can juggle one of my other guests," said the voice.

Irving finished signing the letters. "No problem," he said, half paying attention.

"No problem for you," said the voice.

"Great," said Irving. "What time do you want Bob there?"

"Where will he be staying?"

"The Drake."

"Tell him to call me when he gets in."

"Right," said Irving. "Next time you can do me a favor."

"Essie sends love," said the voice.

"And Mary," said Irving. Essie and Mary were the wives.

The phone clicked off and Irving yelled to his secretary, "Book Mr. Parrish on a night flight to Chicago."

Kup's Show was televised from the seventh floor of the Merchandise Mart Building in Chicago. I arrived early and went to the men's room because I was nervous, and also because I wanted to rehearse a couple of anecdotes and be sure that my thinning hair covered my bald spot. I knew John Wayne would be wearing an expensive hairpiece from one of his movies and I didn't want to look like his father. Luckily the men's room was empty. I stood in front of the mirror and carefully combed my hair. I put the comb in my pocket, smiled, and looked straight into my own eyes.

"Hello, Kup," I said, talking to myself. "It's nice to be on your program." My eyes wandered up to the top of my head. The bald spot still showed. I took out my comb and started over. I back-combed, front-combed, and swirl-combed the few remaining strands of what had once been a luxuriant mane of thick, curly hair. In the past, I had nonchalantly brushed it out of my eyes on some of the fanciest tennis courts, ski slopes, and swimming pools in the western world. Suddenly, quite by accident, the bald spot disappeared. I stopped combing immediately, patted the top of my head, and looked into my eyes again. I pretended that Kup had just asked me a question.

I squinted, smiled a crooked smile, and said, "I was hoping you would ask me that, Kup. As you know, Kup, I devote a full chapter to Mae West in my book, Kup." I then said the name of my book and went into the anecdote about Mae West, glancing up from time to time to see if the bald spot had broken cover. Then I pretended that we were at the end of the program and that Kup had said, "Thank you, Bob Parrish." I shook his imaginary hand and said. "Thank *you*, Kup. Thank you for asking me to be on *Kup's Show*, Kup."

"It's my pleasure," said a voice. I looked over and the real, live Kup was washing his hands next to me. "You must be Bob Parrish," he said.

"Yes, I guess I must," I said. "And you must be Kup, Kup." I thought about shaking his hand again, but I was still holding my comb, and Kup's real hands were soapy.

"Essie read your book and loved it," he said.

Another non-book-buying wife to whose husband my publisher had sent a free, non-royalty-paying copy of my book, I thought. "I'm delighted," I said.

"She particularly liked the part about Charlie Chaplin."

I put my comb away and started to wash my hands. They weren't dirty, but it seemed the friendly thing to do. "Oona Chaplin wrote me a nice letter about that chapter," I said.

Kup dried his hands and came back to look at himself in the mirror. "I liked your Mae West story," he said.

"It'll probably sound better on the program."

"Do you mind though, if I make one suggestion?"

"Of course not," I said, still washing my clean hands.

Kup turned his head slightly but still kept his eyes on himself in the mirror. "Too many 'Kups,'" he said. "You said 'Kup' twenty-one times, and you only said 'Mae West' three times."

"Did I really?" I said. I stopped washing my hands and started wringing them. "Did I really say 'Kup' twenty-one times?"

"That's right," he said, "give or take a Kup or two." He smiled into the mirror and said, "We'd better move along." He started for the door and I dutifully followed, forgetting to dry my hands. As we walked down the hall, he said, "By the way, John Wayne's on the program, so I'll probably ask you about him instead of Mae West."

"No problem," I said. I almost said "Kup" again, but didn't.

One minute before we went on the air, and John Wayne, the star guest, had not arrived. The clock ticked inexorably on, and when the second hand reached twelve, the red light flashed and the announcer said, "This is WMAQ-TV, Chicago." Then he said, "It's time for *Kup's Show.*" One of the cameras, the one with the red light on, zoomed in to a close-up of Kup. I looked down at the little monitor beside my chair.

"Tonight, on our show, we have a Hollywood legend and a friend of his who has written a book about him," said Kup. "John Wayne, Hollywood's longest-lasting star, will tell us about his latest western, *The Shootist,* and Robert Parrish will talk about his new book, in which he recalls his and Big John's early days."

A subliminal close-up of John Wayne saying, "Robert who?" filled my tiny screen. I blinked and it was gone. Only in my mind, I thought.

Kup looked at Wayne's empty chair. "But first, a word from our sponsor," he said. Kup faded from the screen and was replaced by a man with animated pain waves emanating from his sinuses. An unnecessary title saying "Sinus trouble?" flashed on and off, accompanied by a staccato, headache-inducing sound effect.

I looked up from my monitor screen and saw Wayne enter the studio. He was followed by a gaggle of publicity men, journalists, broadcasting assistants, and other hangers-on. He reminded me of a cruiser moving slowly up the Hudson River surrounded by tugs and holiday craft. He was wearing a quizzical smile familiar to millions of fans and a forward-combed hairpiece familiar to his hairdresser. Kup ushered Wayne to his seat just as the sinus-pain waves disappeared and the commercial ended. I cast my eyes down to my monitor and Kup, alone on the screen, said, "Welcome to Chicago, Duke." The picture changed to a shot including Wayne and me. I didn't realize how big Wayne was until I saw myself seated next to him on my little screen.

"Hi, ya, Kup," he said. "I'm glad to . . . be here."

Years ago, I had heard John Ford ask Wayne why he paused in the middle of a sentence, and Wayne had said, "I'm not pausing, I'm just relaxing, getting ready . . . to say the . . . rest of it." Ford told him not to change his delivery, and Wayne never did.

"You and Bob are old friends," said Kup, "so I won't bother to introduce you."

"Hi, ya . . . Bob," said Wayne.

I was so hypnotized by the small screen beside me that I forgot to look up. I said, "Hi, Duke," to the monitor. Kup coughed a theatrical, offstage laugh that must have been a signal to the TV director. The shot of Wayne and me was replaced by a close-up of Kup's face. "We're going to see some scenes from *The Shootist* later in the program," he said, "but first let's talk about Hollywood." The camera moved back to include Wayne, but not me. "Duke, you started working in movies while you were still in college. I believe the late John Ford gave you your first job as a third assistant prop man," said Kup. "Can you tell us what made Ford such a great director and something of what Hollywood was like in those days?"

Wayne picked my book off the table in front of him and held it up. "Will you . . . move the camera up to . . . this book, please," he said. One of the cameras zoomed in, and my book was the only thing on the screen except for John Wayne's big right thumb. "This book'll tell ya . . . more about John Ford and . . . Hollywood than . . . I can tell ya." He put the book down and said, "What's your next question?" I had sent him a copy of the book, but I had no idea whether or not he had read it.

The next question and the next ten or fifteen after that were about *The Shootist*. Then Kup made some kind remarks about my book, and I recited one of the anecdotes that I had rehearsed in the men's room. We watched a few scenes from *The Shootist* and more than a few commercials. We chatted with the other two guests, and in what seemed like a very short time, the program was over. Kup and Wayne had both been very helpful. They had made it seem almost like fun. When the red light went off we all stood up, and the tugboats and the pleasure craft started to move in on the cruiser.

"Duke," I said, "I want to thank you. That was a hell of a nice thing you did, holding the book up."

"I wouldn't have . . . done it if I didn't . . . mean it," he said.

"I sent you a prepublication copy," I said. "Did you get a chance to read it?"

Wayne focused his Johnny Ringo eyes on me, frowned his quizzical smile, and put his big right hand on my shoulder, the same right hand that had hit Monty Clift on the jaw in *Red River*.

"Good to . . . see ya again, Bob," he said. Before I could answer, he turned and headed for the door. His armada steamed after him.

21

Service in the Sun

Generally speaking, the death of an average film director in Hollywood is treated with the same respect, the same excitement, as the death of a junior congressman from South Dakota is treated in Washington. He is mentioned, with his credits and survivors, in the film trade papers (or in the *Congressional Journal*, in the case of the junior congressman). The obituary is usually about ten lines, the last of which says, "He was a member of the Directors Guild of America [or the House of Representatives] for [so many] years." And that's about it.

When Howard Hawks died, the *New York Times* ran a full-column obituary, with photograph. *Newsweek* and *Time* recorded his death in their "Transitions" and "Milestones" departments, and serious cinema journals throughout the world carried on as though Hawks had been Cecil B. DeMille, who is the last person Hawks would have wanted to be, dead or alive. In fact, Hawks was one of the film industry's best filmmakers. A rare specimen: a director who could consistently make films that were equally respected by the critics, the public, and the hardheaded businessmen who finance the production and distribution of motion pictures.

Although known as a "man's director," some of Hawks's biggest hits were made with women stars: *Twentieth Century* (Carole Lombard and John Barrymore), *Bringing Up Baby* (Katharine Hepburn and Cary Grant), *Gentlemen Prefer Blondes* (Marilyn Monroe and Jane Russell), among others.

He discovered Lauren Bacall, teamed her with Humphrey Bogart in *To Have and Have Not,* and Hemingway fans lived happily ever after.

He directed his first picture, *The Road to Glory* (May McAvoy and Rockliffe Fellows), in 1926 and his last, *El Dorado* (John Wayne and Robert Mitchum), in 1967. He averaged a picture a year for forty-one years, including *Scarface, Sergeant York, The Big Sleep,* and *Red River.* He worked with the biggest stars in the business and made millions of dollars for his backers. He was a professional.

On an exceptionally clear, hot December morning, three days after Hawks's death, a long black Cadillac limousine pulled up in front of the All Saints Episcopal Church at Camden Drive and Santa Monica Boulevard in Beverly Hills. Four motorcycle policemen from the Beverly Hills police department's Special Events Division stopped talking to each other and stood at attention beside their motorcycles. An usher, dressed in striped trousers and morning coat, opened the back door of the limousine, and the most famous movie star in the world stepped out. The several hundred people standing behind the ropes on either side of the path to the church murmured, "There he is. . . . He looks great. . . . Better'n he did at John Ford's funeral. . . . That was before his operation. . . . I knew he'd be here . . . ," etc.

John Wayne's face was bronzed and lined the way it was supposed to be, but it was also solemn to suit the occasion. He wore a neat, navy-blue suit on his pain-wracked frame, and on his size-eleven feet he wore neat, two-hundred-dollar cowboy boots. In his first movie, where he had played a bit part, the wardrobe department had outfitted him in boots that were too small for him. He had gone barefooted most of his childhood, and his toes had been allowed to spread out and run free, like the roots of a pecan tree. The undersized, pointed cowboy boots had reined them in and pinched them sardine-like into a leather prison. This caused him to walk on the outside of his feet and lean ahead as though he were going to fall on his face unless he quickly put the next foot forward. He learned to put the next foot forward, and the next, and the next, and after *The Big Trail,* in which he played his first starring role, was released in Paris, a French critic wrote, "Même la démarche de

John Wayne est 'western'." ("Even John Wayne's *walk* is western.")

Nobody spoke at Hawks's service in the church except Wayne. He was led to the pulpit by two churchmen dressed in purple and white robes. The churchmen sat down on a bench at the side and Wayne stood alone, looking at the people who had come to pay their last respects to a fine director. There must have been at least two hundred people in the church, and he seemed to look at each one, personally, before he spoke. There was no music, no coughing or fidgeting, no embarrassment, as his eyes passed from Jimmy Stewart's to Frank Capra's to those of stunt men, wardrobe mistresses, extras, publicity men, relatives, cameramen, friends of all kinds.

Finally, he said, "Howard Hawks . . . was a . . . man. He may not have . . . been a . . . religious man . . . but he was a . . . good man." He paused and then went on with the familiar phrases: "Man that is . . . born of a . . . woman hath but a short . . . time to live and is . . . full of misery. . . ."

After the service was over, the mourners came out into the bright California sunshine. It was here that John Wayne told me that he had read my book. "Bobbie," he said, "that was a . . . fine . . . book you . . . wrote about . . . Pappy Ford. When I go, I hope you . . . or somebody will . . . do the . . . same for me." He had read the book and let me know it.

As the crowd thinned, a dust-covered green Chevrolet with Michigan license plates stopped in front of the church. Two couples peered out. A lady with a blue-rinse hairdo motioned one of the Beverly Hills motorcycle policemen over to the car.

"What's going on, officer?" she asked the policeman.

"It's a funeral, ma'm," he answered.

"Whose?"

"Howard Hawks."

"I never heard of him. What did he do?"

"He died, ma'm. Please move along."

Back in London, I read that Wayne was quite ill and had been taken to the UCLA Medical Center. I sent him a telegram, which was not answered.

Three years later, in a dentist's waiting room in Southampton, Long Island, I picked up a dog-eared magazine whose

cover screamed, BOOK BONUS! JOHN WAYNE: THE MAN
& THE LOVER — TENDER MEMORIES OF HIS LAST ROMANCE.
Inside, a tagline added, "by the woman who shared his life
until the end."

On page 144 of the magazine, I read the following:

> When Duke went to the hospital for the last time, there
> was little fanfare. . . . Something he wrote at this time,
> however, shows how he felt. He had received a cable
> from writer Robert Parrish, who was in London, which
> read: *Dear Duke: Among many others throughout the
> world, my heart is with you. Bob Parrish.*
>
> Duke dictated an immediate reply:
>
> *Dear Bobby: Your thoughtfulness was very much ap-
> preciated. The farther out you go, the lonelier it gets.
> Affectionately, Duke.*
>
> I decided not to send it. I didn't want anybody to find
> out how serious Duke knew his condition was. . . . But his
> words still haunt me: *"The farther out you go, the
> lonelier it gets."*

22

Time to Go Home

Kathie and I sat in the lovely drawing room of our London house. "The leases on this house and the Klosters chalet expire in three years," I said. "Maybe we should start thinking about going home."

"We are home," said my reasonable wife.

"I mean *home* home," I said. "America. Both kids are there. We can't afford a new fifty-six-year lease on this house, and in three years we won't have anything to sell. Out there we could stay in my mother's house until we find a place. I think it's time to start some serious thinking."

"I'll make some serious coffee," said Kathie.

I went to the bar and got out a bottle of Cointreau. When Kathie came back with the coffee I poured a shot into each cup.

"We don't have to rush into anything," I said. "I just believe it's a good idea to start thinking about it."

"I thought about it in the kitchen," said Kathie. "Let's go home."

"I will if you will," I said.

It took us a month to sell the London lease to a nice young man who gave us three months to vacate. Two weeks later we went to Klosters to wrap up the Parrish home away from home away from home.

23

Don't Throw Bouquets at Me . . .

The ads in the local papers read: *Leaving Switzerland — American Style Garage Sale — Bargains! Parrish, Haus Dr. Egger, Klosters.*

When you have lived in London, had a seven-room holiday chalet in Switzerland for twenty years, raised two kids, changed ski gear every time Attenhofer, Head, or Spalding dictated a new design, bought new records when the Beatles and the Rolling Stones segued into Rod Stewart, you collect a lot of stuff. Some of the stuff you are reluctant to part with for sentimental reasons. For example, you remember how you bent that ski pole on the Drostobel run, and you've held on to it for twelve years, never using it, but keeping it to remind you of the most spectacular deep-snow fall of 1964. Its mate, the other, unbent, ski pole, disappeared long ago — somewhere, you don't remember exactly where. But your wife insists on putting the bent pole in the garage sale on a table with an old flat iron, an ashtray from the Argentine Hotel in Dubrovnik, and a brand-new, unopened pair of men's long underwear with the price, SFr 8.20, still on it.

And that's only the beginning. You wind up with the garage packed with everything from bunk beds and other heavy furniture to plastic hair curlers and odd bits of metal that you vaguely associate with a child's tricycle, which, like the unbent ski pole, has long since gone. Maybe they went together. You put your sign on the garage door in three languages and wait for customers.

"Six hundred francs," my wife said. "That should be a good start."

"Sounds fine to me," I said. "A good, round number. What's it for? I mean, where did you get it?"

"The bank," she said. "I got it at the bank. It's for my change. It's what I give the customers when they want to buy something."

"I thought they were supposed to give *you* money," I said. "I thought that's what the sale was about. I thought we were going to get rid of all this junk and have some money instead. You said so yourself."

"We are," said my wife, "but first I have to sell the junk, and to sell it, I have to have some change."

She put the money in a cigar box with some Montecristo number ones, which I kept around for Irwin Shaw.

"Are my cigars part of your change?" I said. "If someone gives you six Upmans and a carton of Marlboros, do you give him one of my two-dollar-and-eighty-five-cent Montecristos' change?"

"I thought the box was empty," she said. "Now why don't you stop standing around looking for trouble and help me put these price tags on." She handed me the cigars and some little round pieces of paper that she had cut out and a Magic Marker. "You take care of the *Grappens,* and I'll do the francs," she said.

"What's *Grappens*?" I asked. "Are you having a wine sale?"

"Irwin Shaw says that's what the Swiss call their coins," she said. "Like pence in England, cents in America, centimes in France, and so on."

"He's crazy," I said. "It's *Rappens.*"

"OK," she said, "I'm not going to argue with you." She handed me the Magic Marker and said, "I'll do them and you do the francs."

"*Was kostet das?*" asked a peculiar voice.

I turned around and there was Johannes, my landlord's seventy-five-year-old gardener. He had a hoe in one hand and a pair of Dior ski goggles in the other. I had bought the ski goggles for my daughter for seventy-five francs, six months before. She wore them twice and then abandoned them in favor of a Givenchy model that cost ninety francs. The Givenchys were also in the sale, along with twenty-eight other pairs of ski goggles.

"Five francs," said my wife.

I blanched visibly and coughed ostentatiously. "What my wife means is that she'll let them go for fifty francs," I said. "Her Swiss-German is not very good and she doesn't know the difference between five and fifty." I bared my teeth with what I thought was a "We men know how silly women are about business, don't we?" smile and added, "She doesn't even know how to spell *Rappen.*"

"*Rappen?*" said Johannes. He was now sure he was on to a hot bargain, so he changed into English and put the goggles on. "How many *Rappen?*" he said.

"They're five francs, Johannes," said my wife, "and they look fine on you." She threw me a deadly look and said, "Get me a piece of paper."

There was no paper around (that's the kind of efficient command post we had set up), so my wife wrote "SFr 5" on the garage door and pointed to it. *"Foof Franken,"* she said to Johannes.

"It's *funf,*" I said.

Johannes took the Diors off and tried on the Givenchys. If he hadn't had a three-day growth of beard and brown, broken teeth, he could have stepped right into, or out of, *Vogue,* or *Harper's Bazaar.* The effect of the upswept goggles was startling.

"Was kostet?" he said. He could speak perfect English, but he switched back and forth to keep me off balance.

Kathie pointed to the "SFr 5" sign on the garage door again. *"Foof Franken,"* she said. *"Alles* ski goggles are *foof Franken."* She threw me a "Why don't you get out of here?" look, so I walked down to the train station to get the *Herald Tribune.* When I got back, Johannes was mowing the lawn. He was still wearing the Givenchy upswepts. The Diors hung around his neck.

"I see you made a sale," I said.

"Yes," said Kathie, "he bought both pairs, but he can't pay until he gets his wages at the end of the day."

"Keep an eye on him," I said.

"I've got everything marked and I'm very optimistic," said Kathie. "I think Johannes is a good omen. We're not even supposed to open until eight o'clock. It's only seven forty-five and we've already made ten francs."

"Yes, darling, that's great. I mean, it really is," I said.

"You don't sound very convincing," she said. "Don't you want to make money out of the sale?"

"Yes, of course I do," I said. "That's the point. That's what I want to talk to you about." I sat down beside her. "Most businesses, even small businesses, work on the profit principle," I said. "I won't bore you with details, but the main idea is to sell things for more than you pay for them. General Motors uses this basic theory. Coca-Cola uses it. Even the Chinese and the Russians use it. It's standard, the world over. Ask anybody."

"What about wear and tear?" she said.

"What about it?"

"Well, when you buy something for a certain price, then wear and tear it for a while, you have to sell it for less than you paid for it. It stands to reason. I'm sure even your big-shot friends would agree to that?"

"What big-shot friends?" I said.

"Those people you just told me about," she said. "General Motors and Coca-Cola and your Chinese and Russian friends. I'm sure even they understand wear and tear."

"Look, darling," I said. "You buy a pair of Dior goggles for seventy-five Swiss francs. Your sixteen-year-old daughter wears and tears them for two runs on the Madrisa on a sunny day. She decides, because of the shape of her teenage face, that she looks better in Givenchy goggles for ninety Swiss francs. Being a dumb-schmuck capitalist-pig American-patsy father, I buy them for her. That is, I buy the Givenchys. I've already bought the goddamn Diors, and my daughter has worn and torn them for two runs. She now wears and tears the Givenchys for one day before she goes back to school. I happen to know what she did on that day. She started at the top of the Gipfel and skied down to the Parsennhutte with six long-haired jerks who yell and scream and keep their skis together. She wasn't even wearing the Givenchys. They were on her arm. How much can you wear and tear a pair of ninety-franc goggles if you don't even look through them?"

"How do you know all this?" said Kathie. "Were you spying on your daughter?"

"I was skiing on the Kreuzweg, just before the Serneus

cutoff, clutching along too fast and wondering how to slow down, when these seven maniacs descended on me and drove me into the bank on the right. I fell and they all jumped over me, screaming like banshees in at least four languages. Kate was number three and she said, 'Hi, Dad,' as she sailed over."

"Who was she skiing with?" said Kathie.

"How the hell do I know?" I said. "I wouldn't have even recognized Kate if she hadn't said 'Hi, Dad' and if I hadn't paid ninety francs for the Givenchys at the Gotchna Sport Shop that morning."

"I hope she wasn't skiing with Stephie Bentinck," said Kathie. "He's wild as can be. She might get hurt."

"Darling, this was six months ago. Kate's now in art school in San Francisco and Stephie's at the Royal Academy of Dramatic Art in London, studying to be an actor. He'll probably make it because he's the sole heir to a thirty-million-dollar fortune. I think it's safe to assume that Kate and her long-haired friends had an accident-free run that day."

"Fine, dear," said my wife. "But let's not talk about the past. Here come some customers."

I looked up and saw three middle-aged Swiss housewives sprinting in our direction. A fourth, chubbier, one brought up the rear. She was puffing heavily and gasping something in Swiss-German — an obscure language, like Basque or Sanskrit. Kathie said she was yelling "Save some American bargains for me," but I interpreted it as "Americans go home."

Kathie had decided to set up her cash desk in front of the garage, in the blazing sun. She explained that women don't like to be watched by other women when they are shopping for bargains. She said they would select what they wanted inside and bring their selections out to her and pay for them. "Just like a supermarket," she said.

I stayed inside, so I was able to observe the mayhem from close range when the ladies swept in. The first three shoppers cleaned off the "Everything on this table, 2 francs" table before the chubby lady wheezed through the garage door. I was particularly interested in the two-franc table because, as a joke, I had slipped in three rocks, two dead flashlight batteries, and a used Brillo pad. Everything went with the first assault wave. Market bags were opened and the junk was thrown in. As they approached the one-franc table, I took my bent ski pole off it and put it against the wall. The lead shopper saw me and asked, *"Was kostet das?"*

"It's not for sale," I said.

She grabbed it and repeated, *"Was kostet das?"*

"Two hundred and twenty-six francs," I said. "It's a unique ski pole. There isn't another ski pole like it in the world."

"Was?" said the Swiss lady.

I took out my Magic Marker and wrote "SFr 226" on the back of my left hand, in green. The lady put on her glasses and studied my hand. She looked at me, birdlike, for a second, then moved in for a close-up of my hand. She muttered something in Swiss-German and then called to one of the other bargain hunters. When her pal arrived, they had a meaningful discussion over the bent ski pole and my green hand. While this was going on, the chubby sprinter raced ahead to the "make an offer" (*Bitte Angebotmachen*) table. The feature of that table was a set of illegal Japanese walkie-talkies. They are not illegal in Japan, but in Switzerland they have to be registered, licensed, taxed, supervised, scrutinized, monitored, and frowned upon. I bought them in one of those fast-shuffle clip joints that occupy temporarily empty stores on Fifth Avenue in New York. They cost me $100 in 1966. I had no idea what I was going to do with them, but they looked like such a bargain that I didn't dare pass them up. I gave the fast-talking New Yorker a $100 bill and he said, "I really shouldn't let them go for this."

"A deal's a deal," I said. I wasn't going to let any New Yorker hustler welsh on me.

The walkie-talkies had remained unused and unloved in our attic in Klosters for ten years. The reasons for this were (a) I had no use for them, and (b) I was scared to death of the Swiss police.

"Was kostet?" said the chubby shopper.

"Two francs," I said. I hated the goddamn things.

When the other ladies heard me say "two francs," they rushed over. "What? What? What is two francs?" they shrieked in Swiss-German.

I decided to play it cool, so I said, "Walkie-talkies. Genuine Japanese illegal one-hundred-dollar walkie-talkies. Two of them." I held up my left hand and extended two fingers.

The chubby shopper looked at the green Magic Marker sign

on my hand and said in Swiss-German, "What is two hundred twenty-six francs?"

The lead shopper said *"Nein, nein"* and a lot of other stuff and grabbed one of the walkie-talkies and made some imaginary police calls in Swiss-German.

The chubby lady snatched the other walkie-talkie and pretended to be a German squad car receiving orders from headquarters. There were no batteries in the walkie-talkies so no sound came out. However, a lot of sound came out of the Swiss shoppers. They talked, they clucked, they scolded, they yelled. It was obvious that they all wanted the illegal walkie-talkies, but they didn't know how to split two walkie-talkies up between four Swiss bargain hunters.

Kathie heard the feverish voices and came into the garage. "Where do you live?" she said to the first lady. She said it in English, because she instinctively knew that all of the women spoke every language, with the possible exception of Urdu.

"Aeuja," said the lady. "I live in Aeuja."

"Where do you live, *Fräulein?*" Kathie asked the fat lady.

"*Frau.* I'm married. I have four children."

"Wonderful," said Kathie. "Where do you and your four children live?"

"With my husband and his mother," said Fatso. "We live with my husband's mother because she owns the house. She's ninety-two years old, and when she dies, the house will belong to Leo."

"Fine," said Kathie. "Where is your ninety-two-year-old mother-in-law's house?"

"In Mombiel," said Fatso. "My husband's family has lived in Mombiel for three hundred years."

"Without a walkie-talkie?" said Kathie. I could have killed her.

"What?" said Fatso.

"I have an idea," said Kathie. "Why don't you each buy a walkie-talkie for one franc, and you can talk to each other from Aeuja to Mombiel?"

"From Memphis to St. Joe," I chirped in helpfully, "wherever the four winds blow."

Kathie glanced at me and raised her left eyebrow. In our thirty-three-year-old marital language, that meant "Please don't say anything when I'm about to get rid of two walkie-talkies that you paid one hundred dollars for ten years ago, and which we have never used once, and which I hate as much as you do."

The fat lady said something to her friend in Swiss-German. The friend nodded.

"OK?" said Kathie.

"*Gut*," said the fat lady.

"*Gut*," said the other lady.

"Make a receipt," said my wife.

"*Jawohl*," said my wife's husband.

The most difficult items to sell in a Swiss garage sale are kids' bunk beds and a Bosch washing machine. I knew the beds were a bargain at 200 Swiss francs. They had cost 900 francs at Möbel Fister in Zurich, but that, of course, was before they had been peed in for fifteen years. I guess that's what Kathie meant by wear and tear. Even so, they were a steal at 200 francs. The garage was now practically empty except for the beds and the washing machine. Kathie was counting her pile of Swiss money for the sixth time.

"How much do the beds cost?" asked a Swiss voice.

I looked up and saw a young man who worked in the local town hall standing beside the bunk beds. The beds were clearly marked "SFr 200." I didn't know how to say "Can't you read?" in Swiss-German, so I pointed to the sign and smiled, hoping he wouldn't smell the mattresses.

He looked at the sign and said something that I couldn't understand. Kathie said, "He says he has two small boys, twins, and they're ready to leave their cradles and move into real beds, and that he is prepared to offer us one hundred francs cash for the beds."

"Ha," I said, and Kathie kicked me. I moved out of range and said, "You make a joke."

The young man looked at me with serious Swiss eyes.

"Ha, ha," I said, in case he hadn't heard my first "ha."

He took out a card with his name and phone number on it. "Hans Weicher," he said. "In case you decide to sell the beds for one hundred francs, please call me."

I said "Ha, ha" again, and then added, "Not a chance. We're not giving them away."

Kathie took the card and said, "Thank you, Mr. Weicher." Mr. Weicher bowed, clicked his heels, and shook Kathie's hand. He didn't shake my hand. Just as well too. Imagine offering 100 lousy Swiss francs for two valuable, slightly worn and torn, peed-in bunk beds. He got in his Mercedes 300 SL and drove away.

"I'd like for him to have them," said Kathie. "He wants them for twins. Don't you think that's cute?"

Before I could tell her how cute I thought it was, the local butcher came in and offered 650 francs for the washing machine. It had cost 1,800 francs two years before and was marked "SFr 900." I said we couldn't let it go for less than 800 francs. Kathie said, "Or seven-fifty," and I went upstairs and built a fire and poured myself a stiff Cherry Heering to avoid another family quarrel.

We had used up all of our decent liquor in anticipation of our exit from Klosters and were now down to dregs of Port, half-bottles of Williamine (a pear brandy also known as Bon Père William), sweet sherry, and fourteen and a half bottles of a deadly local home brew called Rötli. It's a mysterious sweet, syrupy mountain drink that our cleaning woman had given us every Christmas for fifteen years. When she brought it in the first year, the fire was blazing away and "Silent Night" was scratching out for the tenth time on the record player. It was snowing outside, and our two kids were sitting around the tree opening presents. Frau Rachman burst in and said "Merry Christmas!" in Romansch or some such language. We gave her some money and she gave us a bottle of Rötli that she had made herself. She explained that Rötli was a traditional Swiss Christmas drink, and that if you drank it on Christmas Day, you would be healthy for the rest of the year. That was only seven days, so it didn't seem like much of a bargain to me. However, I opened the Rötli and we polished off half the bottle before anyone vomited.

As soon as Frau Rachman left, we took to our beds and weren't able to get up until New Year's Day. Since that first Christmas, not one drop of Rötli has passed our lips. We graciously accepted the well-meant gift each year, and I hid the bottles in a file in my workroom in a drawer labeled "Robert Parrish — Personal." The only other things in that drawer were some blue valium tablets (.3 mg) and nine letters from a Polish girl I had met in Kassel during the war.

Kathie came in with her cigar box and settled down in front of the fire. I asked her if she would like a drink.

"What have we got left?" she said.

"Anything you want," I said. "Just name it. You're the star today."

"Gin martini," she said. "A gin martini in a chilled glass with a lemon peel twisted above it so that you can see the little sprays of fresh lemon oil settling on the surface of the crystalline nectar."

"I didn't know you were a poet," I said.

"Then I would like to sit here by the fire and sip my chilled martini and count my Swiss francs," she said.

"How would you like a Rötli instead?" I said.

"Rötli?" said my favorite shopkeeper. "What in the hell for?"

"For old times' sake," I said. "It's traditional. If we have a nice Rötli, we'll be healthy for the rest of the year, and it's only October. It's a better deal than drinking it at Christmas."

"Not unless you have a stomach pump," she said. "I want a martini."

"It's made of natural ingredients," I said. "It's supposed to be good for you. Swiss hippies drink it."

"Balls," said my finishing school–educated wife. "I've worked like a slave all day and I've made over a thousand dollars. I want a martini."

"How about a Williamine?" I said. She turned around and looked at me. "Or a sweet sherry or a Cherry Heering or a Tabasco or a Fernet Branca or a Worcestershire sauce or a glass of Passuger water," I said. "That's all we have left. That and fourteen and a half bottles of Rötli."

"OK," she said. "I'll have a Rötli, but only if you'll have one with me."

"Right," I said. I opened a 1961 Rötli, filled two wineglasses, and settled down next to my wife on the couch. I handed her a glass and sipped mine. "It's not as bad as I remembered it," I said. "Maybe it's OK if it's fifteen years old." I put my arm around her and pulled her to me. I loved her.

"Would you like a little Williamine with your Rötli?" I said. She didn't answer, so I got the half-bottle of Williamine and topped up our glasses. It looked like sulphur.

Kathie drained her glass with one gulp and said, "Is there any more sticky, sweet Williamine?"

"No, darling," I said, "but how about some sticky, sweet sherry?"

"I'd rather have Port, Port and Rötli." She pursed her lips the way she did when she was starting to get drunk. I emptied the dregs of the Port into her glass and added some more Rötli.

"Cheers," she said, and dribbled a few drops of the mixture on her blue jeans before she found her mouth. The spots smoked a little bit and then turned snow-white.

"Cheers," I said, trying manfully not to be sick.

We drank silently for a while, up to 1964, Rötli-wise, and finally finished off the bottle of Cherry Heering. I think it mixed better with the Rötli than the rest of the stuff.

Kathie was now quite loaded and she was staring at the fire. Her face glowed in its reflection, and a large tear inched its way down her cheek. I put my arm back around her, and she leaned her head on my shoulder and cried for a while without shaking or moaning or grimacing or doing any of the things that wives usually do when they cry. It was one of the things I had always liked about Kathie. She could cry with the best of them and never make any fuss. After a while she said, "I want those cute twins to have the bunk beds."

"How do you know they're cute?" I said. "You've never seen them."

"All twins are cute," she said. She wiped her face and took Mr. Weicher's card from her purse. She went to the phone and dialed his home number. "Is Mr. Weicher there?" she said. After a pause she said, "It's Mrs. Parrish, the lady with the bed. Mr. Weicher was with me this afternoon. I wanted to ask him when he could come back, and . . ." There was another pause, a longer one this time. Finally my wife said, "Thank you, Mrs. Weicher. My number is four-one-eight-three-two." She hung up, turned to me, and said, "That was his wife. She didn't sound very friendly."

"How would *you* sound if a strange drunk called and said she had a bed and had been with your husband and wanted him to come back?" I said.

The phone rang and Kathie picked it up. "Oh, hello, Mr. Weicher," she said. "I called to say that you can have the bunk beds and mattresses for your twins for one hundred francs." Pause. "Oh." Pause. "She did?" Pause. "I see." Pause. "Yes, well, could you hold on for a moment?" Kathie put her hand over the phone and said, "Mr. Weicher's wife says he should only pay eighty francs for the bunk beds. What do you think?"

"I think Mrs. Weicher is a shrewd cookie," I said.

"Be serious," slurred Kathie. "The moving people will be here tomorrow to take our good furniture to storage, and if we don't take this offer, we're going to be stuck with the beds. I think we should grab it."

"So tell Mr. Weicher you accept his generous offer, and be prepared for him to beat you out of another twenty francs when he comes to pick up the beds in the morning."

"Hello, Mr. Weicher," Kathie said. "You can have the beds for eighty francs." Pause. "Yes, thank you. Goodnight." She hung up the phone and came back to the fire. "Well, that's that," she said. "Eighty francs is better than two bunk beds with soggy mattresses."

"Right on," I said.

"Now there's only one thing left," she said. "That washing machine. That's your baby. I sold the beds; you can sell the washing machine. Call the butcher in the morning and tell him you'll let him have it for seven hundred francs. If he hesitates, tell him six-fifty, then six, five, four, three, and so on."

"You're a tough bargainer," I said. "The guy's already said he'd give us six hundred and fifty francs for it, and you're telling me to sell it to him for 'six, five, four, three, and so on'!"

"Maybe his wife won't let him pay six-fifty," she said. "Maybe she'll be like Mr. Weicher's wife."

"Then he doesn't get the washing machine," I said. "It's a steal at six-fifty. Otherwise his wife can keep washing his butcher's aprons by hand."

"He's a very nice man," said Kathie.

I poured us each another Rötli.

"I know his wife," she said. "They have four kids. Have you any idea how much laundry four kids can come up with each day?" she said.

"Drink your Rötli," I said.

"Drink yours," she said. She was getting aggressive.

"I don't feel so well," I said. "I think I'll go to bed." I stood up and looked at her sitting by the fire. "Are you coming?" I said.

"I'll be along in a minute," she said. "I want to count our profits." She stretched out on the green and blue hearthrug in front of the fire and dumped the cigar box full of money on the beautiful polished parquet floor.

At 7:03 the next morning, a giant moving van from Gebr. Kuoni: Chur, AG pulled up in front of our chalet. Three strong, efficient men started to move our good furniture into the van. They were miracle workers. I have never seen anyone do so much in such a short time. At 11:30 they had most of the contents packed and carefully stowed in their van.

I had swept out the garage and tried to move the washing machine to the front so that prospective buyers could see it. I couldn't budge it. Swiss washing machines (and all washing machines, as far as I know) have a cement base (a) to keep them steady when they are in action chewing up your clothes and (b) to keep elderly husbands from moving them to the front of Swiss garages. I asked one of the Kuoni men to help me. He was about twenty-five years old and looked like an Olympic weight lifter. We couldn't move the washing machine an inch. While we were trying to catch our breath, the butcher pulled up in his Volkswagen.

"*Guten Tag*," said the butcher.

"*Ah, guten Tag*," I said. Then I added, "Good morning, Herr Butcher." The Kuoni man went about his business.

"I have been discussing the washing machine with my wife," said the butcher.

"So have I," I said. "That is, I have been discussing it with *my* wife."

"My wife says we'll take the washing machine but we can only pay five hundred francs." He laughed a little and then said, "I told her I had offered six hundred and fifty francs and that you had not accepted the offer, so she said I should offer you five hundred francs. You know how wives are."

"Yes, I do," I said. "It's funny you should say that, because while your wife was cutting the price of my washing machine, my wife was raising the price. When you didn't accept her special rock-bottom offer of seven-fifty last night, she said, 'That washing machine is practically new. Raise the price back to nine hundred francs and don't take a *Rappen* less.'"

"How old is the machine?" said the butcher.

"We bought it from Dat Wyler, the electrical store, for eighteen hundred francs two years ago," I said. "I can show you the bill."

"I can give you six hundred francs," he said.

"Nine hundred," I said.

"Six-fifty, if you promise not to tell my wife," he said.

"Eight-fifty, if you promise not to tell mine," I said.

"Seven," he said.

"Eight."

"Seven-fifty."

"Seven-seventy-five."

"Seven-fifty is as high as I can go."

"Seven-seventy-five is as low as I can go. Take it or leave it."

"*Was?*" he said. After all the intense bargaining, he suddenly couldn't understand English.

"If you want it for seven hundred and seventy-five francs, it's yours," I said. "Take it away." I knew he couldn't take it away without a low-bed tank retriever, but I didn't tell him that.

"Seven hundred and fifty francs," he said. He took out a pencil and wrote "SFr 750" on the back of an order for two pounds of bacon and a rack of lamb.

"No," I said. I took his pencil and wrote "SFr 775" and handed him back his pencil and his order book. He put them both in his pocket and walked away. He didn't say "No" or "*Nein*" or "Are you crazy?" or "My wife won't let me" or "I'll think it over" or anything else. He just walked over to his Volkswagen and drove away.

I fought back an impulse to kick the Bosch washing machine with its cement base. The Kuoni men were putting the last of our Graubünder furniture in the moving van.

"I beg your pardon," I said, "but would you fellows please put this washing machine in my Volkswagen Varient 1600 station wagon?"

The three Kuoni men looked at the machine, and the one who had tried to help me before said, "It's bolted to the floor."

"No," I said. "It's just heavy. I'm sure you can get it into the station wagon if all three of you really put your minds and your backs to it." They got some wide web straps and put them over their shoulders and somehow got the washing machine into the back of the station wagon just as my wife arrived to pack the car for the trip back to London.

"Why are they putting the washing machine in the car?" she said. "I thought you were going to sell it to the butcher."

"It didn't work out," I said.

One of the Kuoni men said something in Swiss-German and pointed to the back tires of the station wagon, which were now half-flat.

"The washing machine's too heavy," said Kathie. "The Volkswagen can't take it. We'll break the springs."

"Nonsense," I said. "The VW can take anything. We just need to put a bit more air in the tires." I thought I saw the Kuoni man roll his eyes, but I wasn't sure.

"But what are we going to do with it?" said Kathie. "We'll get a new washing machine in America."

"I'm not going to practically donate a perfectly good washing machine to a crooked Swiss butcher and his wife just because they think they have us over a barrel," I said. "I'd rather take it to America and give it to the Salvation Army."

"What about the different cycle and the voltage and the customs and all that?" said my wife.

"I'll handle it," I said. I gave each of the Kuoni men twenty francs, and we drove our overloaded Volkswagen to Mr. Kaufman's garage.

Mr. Kaufman filled the tank, then filled the tires, then shook his head. He looked in the back of the station wagon and said, "You must be smuggling gold. What is so heavy?"

"My wife," I said. "It's the Swiss cooking."

"You better check the tires from time to time," he said. "I think you have too much weight."

"Thank you, Mr. Kaufman, I'll do that," I said.

Kathie and I started down the long descent to Landquart. I don't think I've ever seen the Klosters Valley so beautiful. It had snowed the night before and the snow covered the high mountains, but the trees in the valley with their stunning fall colors were sparkling in the morning sun.

"Do you think we'll ever come back?" said Kathie.

"Sure," I said. The car felt rather strange on the turns.

"We've been coming here for over twenty years," said Kathie. "Some of our best friends are here."

I shifted into a lower gear and wished I had sold the washing machine to the butcher. "So we'll come back to see them," I said.

"We won't, you know," said my wife.

There was definitely something wrong with the way the Volkswagen was handling. "Why not?" I said. "Why do you say we won't come back and see our friends?" I tried the brakes.

"Because it's the end of an era," she said. "When eras end you don't go back and see what's happened to them. You move on. You live your life. That's why we're going back to America."

The brakes worked, but the back end of the car swayed around unnaturally. "We can come back and stay at the Chesa Grischuna," I said. "You can have breakfast in bed."

"It won't be the same," said Kathie. The back of the Volkswagen was now whipping around like a roller coaster. Kathie pretended she didn't notice it. "You can't recapture the past," she said. I saw a filling station on the right side of the road and pulled in. "Why are we stopping?" said my wife.

"I want to check the tires," I said. I got out and saw that both of the back tires were almost flat. They were new tires, so I knew that the trouble must be the overloading of the Volkswagen with the goddamn washing machine.

"We've got to get rid of the washing machine," I said. "It's too heavy. The car won't take it."

Instead of saying "I told you so," my wife said, "What'll we do?" That's why the marriage had lasted thirty-three years.

"You phone Kuoni in Zurich and tell them that we'll leave the washing machine with them this afternoon," I said. "Tell 'em it's an emergency."

"Do you think they'll take it?" she said.

"Of course they'll take it," I said. "You pay them lots of money and they take things. That's their business."

"Even on Saturday?" she said. "We won't be in Zurich until after noon, and they'll probably be closed."

"*Guten Tag,*" said the gas-station attendant.

"Do you speak English?" I said.

"At your service," he said.

"I have a Bosch washing machine in perfect condition in the back of this car," I said. I pointed in through the window.

"At your service," he said again.

"Well, now," I said. "The machine is quite valuable, but I'm prepared to let it go for far less than it's worth because it seems to be too heavy for the Volkswagen." I pointed to the beleaguered tires.

"At your service," said the attendant. He got the tire-inflating machine and proceeded to pump up all of the tires. I followed him around.

"My wife bought it two years ago at Dat Wyler's and it's barely been used," I said. "We only come to Switzerland for holidays."

He looked up and said something in Swiss-German. It seemed to be about how much pressure I wanted in the tires, so I said, "*Ja, gut.*" He gave the left rear tire another shot of Swiss air and dragged his little piece of equipment up to the front of the car. I looked around and saw that Kathie was doing a crossword puzzle. I knelt down beside the attendant.

"Look," I said. I didn't whisper, but I lowered my voice, like a racetrack tout. "I'm going to be frank with you. My wife and I have had a disagreement about the washing machine. She thinks I should have sold it to Mr. Kaiser, the butcher, in Klosters. For various reasons that I won't bore you with, I disagreed. I decided to take it to London. Now I find that it's too heavy for the Volkswagen." I pointed to the tire. The attendant gave it another squirt. "If you'll get a couple of your friends to help you unload the washing machine, you can have it, free. It won't cost you a cent." He looked up and smiled. I smiled back.

"At your service," he said.

I suddenly realized that those were the only three English words I had heard him say. "Kiss my ass," I said.

"At your service," he replied.

"And go to hell," I added.

"At your service," he repeated.

"Are you sure you speak English?" I asked.

He finished inflating the last tire, smiled, and said "At your service" again. I gave him a franc, got in the car, and pulled out into the mainstream of traffic headed toward Zurich. It had started to rain. Not a nice, little, misty, poetic shower — a sudden Swiss downpour.

I drove as fast as I dared under the circumstances and arrived at the Kuoni office in Zurich at five minutes after twelve. As I stood in the rain, the watchman pointed to four signs, which gave the office hours in four languages. The English sign said CLOSED 12:00 NOON SATURDAY," and as far as I could tell, the other signs said the same thing in German, French, and Italian. I asked the watchman if he spoke English and he said, "*Nein.*" I asked him if he wanted a washing machine and Kathie said, "I think we're wasting time."

"Why?" I said.

"He doesn't look like a washing-machine buyer," she said.

"What does a washing-machine buyer look like?" I asked.

"I don't know," she said. This took me by surprise because, after the opening I had given her, I thought she was going to say "Like a butcher." I got in the car and slammed the door. "Let's drive around and see if we can find someone who might take it off our hands," she said.

"Everything's closed," I said.

"We're almost out of gas," said Kathie. "Let's go to a gas station where they speak English and ask if they know anyone who wants to buy a washing machine." The tires were almost flat again, too.

Six blocks from the Kuoni office, we came to a huge used-car lot. There must have been five hundred used cars of all makes with small red-and-white banners hanging forlornly from the radio antennas of each one. In the back, between a Mercedes 240 and an Alpha Romeo, was a run-down two-wheel trailer that served as an office. On the top of the trailer was a sign that said OCCASIONS — WIR KAUFEN UND VERKAUFEN.

"*Occasions!*" said Kathie. "That's French and it means 'opportunities.' Pull in."

"It means they're trying to sell their used cars," I said. "It doesn't mean they want to buy a used washing machine."

"Don't be silly," said Kathie. "Pull in. I have a hunch about this place. Besides, I have to go to the bathroom."

When little girls are about four years old, they learn that if they say they have to "go to the bathroom," responsible grown-ups have to arrange for them to go to the bathroom. Only an exceptionally brave parent says, "I don't believe you," unless he is prepared to cope with a stained front seat or a flooded church pew or a soggy cinema seat.

"It's a used-car lot," I said, "not a public toilet."

"There's a gas station next to it," she said. "Pull in."

I did as I was told, and when the Volkswagen groaned to a stop, Kathie jumped out and ran through the rain to the ladies' room. That's what you have to watch out for. Sometimes they actually *do* have to "go to the bathroom." I told the attendant to fill the tank with Total (regular) and check the tires, and I hurried over to the trailer-office.

A very good-looking young man said, in perfect English, "Some weather, eh? Like England. What can I do for you?" I remembered my experience with the "At your service" fellow and thought, Maybe this guy will keep saying "Some weather, eh? Like England. What can I do for you?" over and over again, so I said, "How's the rest of your English?"

"I beg your pardon?" he said.

"Ah," I said. "You speak English."

"Yes, I do," he said. "I went to the London School of Economics for three years."

"Then you're my man," I said. "You'll understand my problem."

"Please sit down," he said.

I sat in a comfortable canvas chair and told him about the washing machine. I told him about the tires and the springs on the Volkswagen and the cement in the washing machine and the fact that we could buy a new washing machine in America.

He listened patiently, and when I finished he said, "Yes, I see. I sympathize with you. I understand your problem. The thing is, though," he said, "we are in the used-car business, not the washing-machine business. How much mileage do you have on the Volkswagen?"

"More than I have on the washing machine," I said.

"I could probably let you have two thousand, five hundred francs if the tires are in good shape," he said.

"They'll be OK if I get rid of the washing machine," I said. I took out a brand-new one-hundred-franc note and put it on his desk.

"What's that?" he said.

"It's a brand-new one-hundred-franc note," I said. "It's yours if you'll take the washing machine off my hands and not tell my wife the terms of our deal."

"Does the washing machine belong to you or to your wife?" he said.

I put another fifty francs on the desk and reached in my pocket and put a handful of coins on top of the two notes. "That's it," I said. "That's all I've got." I must have looked as though I were going to burst into tears, because his big Swiss heart melted. He put the two notes in his wallet and started to count the change. His hands moved like a conjurer's or an experienced bank teller's. He quickly separated the five-franc pieces, the two francs, the one francs, and the various other coins. He counted them and they came to SFr 18.75. He handed me back two coins.

"This is English money," he said.

"Oh. I'm sorry," I said. "I didn't realize . . . I mean, I wasn't trying to unload sterling on you." The Swiss were not too crazy about the British pound in those days, and I saw my deal going down the drain. I picked up the two tenpenny coins and put them in my pocket. "I'll make it up to you," I said. "I can give you a check on the Swiss Credit Bank for the equivalent amount."

"Forget it," he said. "I'm glad to help you out." As I suspected, he was all heart. "Let's go get the washing machine."

We dashed through the rain to the gas station, where he got three mechanics to help him unload the washing machine. He paid them each a franc of my money and told them to put the washing machine in the back end of his trailer-office. I shook his hand, and as we drove away I looked back through my rearview mirror. The front end of the trailer-office was two feet in the air and the back end was on the ground. The used-car dealer from the London School of Economics was standing in the rain and waving his arms and yelling at the three mechanics.

"The rain has stopped," said Kathie.

I turned the windshield wipers off. "That's because we got rid of the you-know-what and we're out of Switzerland," I said.

"Don't be unfair," she said. "We had some of our best years there."

The sun came out and made a French rainbow. We were driving through the Doubs valley between Besançon and Beaune. Route 73 curved along the river Doubs, and the Volkswagen was no longer swaying from side to side. We had a reservation at the Hôtel de la Poste in Beaune that night, where we would get the best wine France had to offer and a meal that was too good for us. I was sitting next to the person I loved most in the world, and she said, "Why didn't the butcher buy the washing machine? How much did he offer?"

I turned on the radio and concentrated on tuning it in to Radio Luxembourg.

"Were you able to make a better deal with the fellow in Zurich?" she said. "He seemed nice. Spoke perfect English."

"I think I can get the World Series on the Armed Forces Network," I said. I turned up the volume and almost blasted us both out of the car with an Austrian military band. I turned it down.

"He probably has kids," said Kathie. "That's why he bought the washing machine. How much did he pay?"

The band music finished. "Shhh," I said, "I think this is it." I turned up the volume. An Austrian voice said something that I didn't understand and then said "Oklahoma." The overture of the original score of the Rodgers and Hammerstein musical burst out of the Volkswagen's Blaupunkt radio. "Ok-la-homa! Where the wind comes sweepin' down the plain. . . ."

This was "our" song, "our" musical score, "our" 1943 wedding music. We had seen the show in New York the night before we were married. The war was on and we were in love. Since then, every time either of us heard any of the music from *Oklahoma!* we got sentimental and looked around for each other.

"Don't throw bouquets at me — Don't please my folks too much . . ." — I turned the Blaupunkt up — "Don't laugh at my jokes too much — People will say we're in love!"

Kathie put her head on my shoulder and sang the lyrics along with Shirley Jones. " 'Don't take my arm too much,' " she sang. " 'Don't keep your hand in mine . . .' " — she put her hand on the steering wheel on top of mine — " 'Your hand feels so grand in mine,' " she sang, and pressed my hand. " 'People will say we're in love!' " I gripped the wheel for all I was worth and aimed for the French rainbow.

24

The Past Is a Good
Place to Visit . . .

When we returned to London, we plunged into packing and deciding what to keep and what to sell. In the middle of one of these discussions, my brother, Gordon, phoned from Los Angeles and suggested that I come out and see my mother. "She talks about you and I think you should come out," he said. I left on the next plane.

For sixty years my mother had rubbed elbows with some of the most famous people in the world. A short list would include Charlie Chaplin, John Gilbert, Clark Gable, Judy Garland, Laurel and Hardy, Marilyn Monroe, and Frank Sinatra. Mother was a film extra, a charter member of the Motion Picture Screen Extras Guild. Two years before, on her ninetieth birthday, she was admitted to the Van Nuys Convalescent Hospital at 6250 Peach Street, fifty yards from the San Diego Freeway in the San Fernando Valley. As you turn west off Sepulveda Boulevard, there is a sign that says NOT A THROUGH STREET. Next to the hospital on one side there is a Seventh Day Adventist church. On the other side is a place that sells trailers and mobile homes ("Over 300 Homes Away From Home on the Premises"). Mother never saw the signs, nor either of the establishments, because she was in a drugged sleep when she was brought into the hospital.

She later told me that at 4:15, when she woke up that first morning there, all she could see was the television set, which was strategically placed halfway up the wall opposite the two beds in her semiprivate room. She said she had opened her eyes and there, on the twenty-six-inch screen, was an "Our Gang" comedy in which I had acted when I was ten years old.

There was no sound coming from the TV screen because each evening at 10:00, Dr. Erickson, the manager of the hospital, turned off the sound in all of the seventeen rooms with a master switch. He left the picture on because he felt that it might have a soothing effect on a waking patient and need not disturb a sleeping patient. Mother said she had watched me take a slice of watermelon from Farina, the black boy in "Our Gang," and throw it at Joe Cobb, the fat boy. Joe ducked and the watermelon splattered on the face of a policeman who happened to be standing behind Joe.

"The policeman raised his club and took off after you and the other kids in the gang," she said. "You all separated and ran in different directions. The policeman stopped and scratched his head. Then, as he stomped his foot, he slowly disappeared. The screen went black for a few seconds and the words *The End* faded in and then faded out.

"I loved it," she said.

I decided to go directly from the airport to the hospital to see my mother, and check in at my hotel later. I quickly crossed the fifteen feet of blast-furnace heat between the air-conditioned taxi and the air-conditioned hospital. The hospital was quite cheerful. There were skylights, clean floors, bright curtains, wide halls, Muzak.

As I entered my mother's room, I was assaulted by the sound of sirens, screaming tires, and gunshots. My mother and another old lady were sleeping soundly through a *Kojak* rerun. I turned off the sound on the TV set and sat down beside my mother. She was breathing regularly and looked quite peaceful. I took her hand in mine, and when she didn't wake up, I closed my eyes and dozed off into a deep, jet-lag sleep.

I was awakened by a soft pressure on my hand and my mother's voice saying, "My son." At first I thought I was dreaming. I slowly opened my eyes. Kojak held a snub-nosed .38-calibre pistol in both hands. The .38 was aimed straight at me, and Kojak was screaming hysterically, but instead of Kojak's familiar snarl, I heard my mother's voice.

"Oh, son," she said, "I'm so glad you're here." I turned away from the TV set before Kojak pulled the trigger. My mother was wide awake. Her wise, beautiful eyes were sharp, clear — not what I had expected. She tightened her grip on my hand.

"I knew you'd come," she said. She told me, again, about waking up and seeing me in the fifty-year-old "Our Gang" comedy on TV two years ago, and about her doctor, whom she liked. She told me about her favorite nurse, Eleanor, and about her roommate, Miriam Dawson. She and Miriam both had remote-control buttons for the TV set at the bedside, but Miriam, who had been a wardrobe mistress at Universal for twenty-six years, had more strength to push the buttons, so her choice was usually on the screen. Miriam was a Dodgers baseball fan and she liked some Humphrey Bogart movies, but not all of them. John Wayne was her all-time favorite, my mother told me, except for maybe Charles Farrell in *Seventh Heaven* or John Gilbert in *The Big Parade*, especially in the scene where Renée Adorée runs along beside the truck that is taking him off to the front in the First World War.

"I knew you'd come," my mother said again. Her eyes fluttered, her hand went limp, and she drifted off to sleep and never woke up.

I went back to my mother's house and called Kathie. She wanted to come right out, but I convinced her to wait for me in London, that I would return in a few days.

After twenty years, I was back where I grew up, where I thought I belonged. But everything had changed, including me. Now I didn't know where I belonged.

25

The State of the Art

At the Hollywood studios, the old heavyweights had all been replaced by new heavyweights, and the new heavyweights had been replaced by newer heavyweights several times. Movies still came out of the studios and money still came in. That's what it was all about before I went away, and, from a practical point of view, that's what it's all about today. The same old ball game, except it was different. The main difference, of course, was in not being young and "on the make."

My friend Irwin Shaw heard about my mother's death and called me in Hollywood from his new home in Southampton, Long Island.

"I've just talked to Kathie, Bobbie," he said. "I'm sorry about your mother." He waited a short time for me to answer, then he said, "Now look, Bobbie. You're going to meet Kathie here Saturday. It's all arranged. The weather's beautiful and we've got plenty of room. You can stay with us as long as you like. We'll meet you at the airport."

I accepted my ex-partner's generous invitation, and everything was as he had promised. He and Marian and Kathie met me at the airport, the weather was perfect, and, as usual, the Shaws had a delightful guest room and were perfect hosts. They made us forget about Hollywood, London, and Klosters.

Kathie and I drove to Montauk Point, back to Riverhead, out to Orient Point, then took a ferry to Shelter Island, in the middle of Long Island Sound. After lunch we took another ferry across to Sag Harbor, a charming old whaling village. We had a drink at the Long Wharf Bar, overlooking the harbor, and Kathie said, "This is a lovely part of the world." We had another drink and she said, "Wouldn't this be a fine place to start the third act of our lives?"

"We have no friends here," I said.

"We have Irwin, and Gloria Jones," she said. "They know everybody. It would be a fresh start."

"What would we do every day?"

"You can make documentary movies and write another book. I'll plant a garden and write poetry, and we'll live happily ever after."

We found a house overlooking Gardiner's Bay, furnished it with leftovers from Hollywood, London, and Klosters, moved in, and met some wonderful people. Kathie planted a garden and started writing poetry. I made a documentary film with Bertrand Tavernier, a close friend from France, and I've just finished writing a new book titled *Hollywood Doesn't Live Here Anymore.*

Index